A FIELD GUIDE TO

Mysterious

PLACES OF THE WEST

Stone sphere in 150-million-year-old sandstone, Morrison, Colorado. Student researcher Margaret Hoover looks on.

A FIELD GUIDE TO

Mysterious
Places of the West

SALVATORE M. TRENTO

PRUETT PUBLISHING COMPANY
BOULDER, COLORADO

Printed in the United States
10 9 8 7 6 5 4 3 2 1

Library of Congress Cataloging-in-Publication Data

Trento, Salvatore Michael.
      A field guide to mysterious places of the West: how to get to strange, weird, and unusual sites / Salvatore Michael Trento.
          p.   cm..
      Includes bibliographical references (p.) and index.
      ISBN 0-87108-851-7 (acid-free)
      1. West (U.S.)—Guidebooks. 2. Curiosities and wonders—West
(U.S.)—Guidebooks. I. Title.
F590.3.T74   1994
917.804'33—dc20   94-31898
                                                      CIP

Contents

3 New Mexico

Acknowledgments

Many people over many years helped produce this book. The original crew of the Middletown Archeological Research Center in southern New York and New England got everything going. Thanks to Cathy Bookey for showing me glacial anomalies early on. I thank all of my former undergraduate and graduate students at Lesley College and the University of Massachusetts for keeping the thrill of anomalies alive and well. This book's format was sketched out at Grendel's Tavern in Harvard Square after an evening geology class.

Many of my former students in Denver must also be thanked for helping: Margaret Hoover, John Rice, Jon Right, Anna Cayton-Holland, Brian Monaghan, Hisatake Kamori, Ryan O' Shaughnessy, Anne Drabkin, Colin Kronewitter, Jennifer Person, and Rachel Miller all assisted in a variety of ways.

Also to my colleagues at Graland, who helped me far more than they realize. Thanks to Nancy Priest, John Threlkeld, Jan Bacuum, Tony Gerlicz, Larry Dougherty, Tony Cantanese, Kathey Stokes, Tom Rice, Andrean Andrus, and Charles Elbot.

Special thanks must go to Doug Miller, who led me to the Hogback Ruins, the Dutch Creek Inscribed Cave, and the Sandstone Cave. To Richard Right I'm also indebted for hiking around with me one hot June day and helping me find a standing stone.

Thanks to Dale Green for use of his Lehman Caves map, and to Alvin McLane for his scholarly study of the Cave Valley Cave.

Thanks to Bill McGlone, who is the expert on Colorado anomalies. Bill's

The Badlands of South Dakota. (Reprinted from Winchell, *Sketches of Creation*)

pioneering work on American inscriptions is the pedagogical baseline by which all other work must be judged.

Thanks to George Robinson of Taos, New Mexico, for help in securing many of the prints and maps used in this book.

Thanks to my Bermuda comrade, Maria Maruisch, who has caved, dived, climbed, and accompanied me on all sorts of adventures, including a jaunt to a golden mountain in western Massachusetts and to those strange "Pudding Stones" in Roxbury: What a long, strange trip it's been. Thanks for listening and putting up with this stuff.

And finally, one thousand and one thanks to Leslie, Reane, and Sarah for those endless afternoons of fun in the Rockies.

Introduction

Some regions of the world evoke a kind, gentle feeling. The air is clearer, the sunlight is brighter, the people seem more pleasant There are other places, however, where chaos and fear seem to loom. A gloomy, oppressive feeling hovers over all inhabitants. Some locales are remarkably inspirational while, elsewhere, muddled thought is pervasive. Why should this be? Does mere topography or climate influence human mood?

Over the years much has been written about such places with respect to geology, landforms, ecosystems, and the weather. There are a host of scientific studies that relate barometric pressure, dense cloud cover, rainy days, and other climatological variables to human behavior. More recently, certain New Age thinkers have explained the phenomena in more ethereal, less tangible terms: the so-called earth energy paradigm. The idea is that the planet, through various geological faults and cracks in the crust, leaks "good" or "bad" energy. According to this concept, people are affected in positive or negative ways, depending upon the nature of the energy. Although it is tempting to believe this idea, it does little to explain what the "energy" actually is and what makes it positive or negative.

But whatever the explanation, mysterious places do indeed exist. And they are found throughout the world. In the late 1970s I put together a research team to survey an odd assortment of mysterious stone ruins that are scattered throughout the U.S. In a report about our work I detailed the results of eighteen months of identifying, surveying, and categorizing the fields and byways of rural America. I not only described the bizarre, inexplicable ruins we found and excavated, but put into context mysterious stonework dating back in some cases thousands of years.

During the course of the investigation I visited many rural people: western ranchers, country farmers, woodsmen from Maine, hunters from Tennessee, and rangers who led me to partially uncovered ruins. After our team fully recorded a site, we often stayed with these people, sharing dinner and travel tales with them. Inevitably, these kind folks would say, "If you thought that jumble of stone was something, then you should see what's over the next ridge! But be careful, the place is weird." Most of these people couldn't (or wouldn't) fully explain what they meant.

Invariably, we didn't have time to hike the next ridge, or else the description seemed too strange or peculiar. But as our fieldwork continued, the unusual accounts increased. A few years later, intrigued by the stories and their possibilities, I decided to look into these fanciful tales. What I found were honest to goodness mysteries, true anomalies.

Anomalies are things or events that can't be explained in a rational way. They are deviations from the norm: the odd, the peculiar, the strange. Anomalies contradict current scientific thought and therefore are intriguing. For example, stories about Bigfoot (a giant, humanlike hominid in the American Northwest), the Loch Ness Monster (a large lake creature from northern Scotland), UFO abduction accounts, crop circles in English wheat fields, and even people swearing they saw Elvis at the local K-Mart are interesting for three very different reasons:

1. The stories are absurdly funny and we all like a good laugh.
2. The stories are hoaxes. It is interesting that many people can be duped in our modern world of computers and twenty-four-hour news. This is surely a testament to our collective need to believe weird things. P. T. Barnum would be delighted.
3. And finally, maybe the stories contain some element of truth. Is it possible that some of these things really have happened? (Well, perhaps not Elvis...) Does the world still hold secrets waiting to be uncovered? Could there really be places where strange and unusual things happen to all who pass through? Perhaps our earth, this planet, still has more unfamiliar terrain than we have reckoned.

This guide is a collection of strange places and things I have examined. Its objective is to provide readers with a wide selection of descriptions and directions to unusual geological and archeological sites. It describes a locale

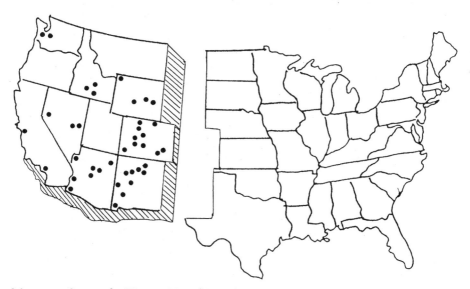

Mysterious Sites in the Western United States

in detail. It lists how to get there, and it offers the best available explanation about the site. Whenever possible, the latest research and thought on anomalies are included. Where scientific study or reports are limited, local interpretations and anecdotes are used.

Should you wish to visit the places listed in this book, then do take the time to contact the person or organization listed with each description. Although a good many months were spent collecting data, drawing maps, and so on, things change. Property is bought, sold, and developed. Holes are dug, trees are cut, landscapes reshaped. It can be maddening to hike around the mountains for hours and see nothing. Also, it can be illegal. Securing permission to walk on posted private property is an essential first step to all field observation.

When a site is on public land, there is a good chance that a National Park Service area is nearby. Either contact the specific park listed for the site, or, if it is not mentioned, write or call for information: U. S. Department of Interior, National Park Service, P.O. Box 37127, Washington, D.C. 20013-7127; (202) 208- 4747.

There will be some who abhor a field guide that details how to get to various sites. The reasoning goes something like this: If the public knows about these places they will inevitably destroy them; protection means keeping sites out of the public eye. Although there is no doubt that some people do vandalize things—from city buses to ballpark bathrooms—most do not. To keep the locations of these amazing places secret is to defeat the very thing most scholars yearn for: public awareness and respect of unusual and ancient places. The more people know about these sites, the more educated the public will become about such matters, and the more our shared past will be appreciated and protected. To keep these sites hidden in obscure journals (and sometimes only referred to in code!) is to deny the layperson the opportunity to understand our wondrous past.

So prepare yourself for a journey into the unknown world of the mysterious and the strange. Some of the sites I have visited evoke happy feelings while others seem odd and fearful. Either way, all are guaranteed to astound and amaze those who venture in search of mysterious places.

1

History and Background

Throughout the world there are many mysterious places. From earliest times, people were drawn to certain locales where they probably felt something special. When archeologists examine a two-thousand-year-old set of upright stone circles in southeastern Colorado, for example, looking for some reason why they exist, they find none. The purpose of the stones and *why* they were placed where they stand is not known. And yet, the more we examine ancient structures built by humans, the more it is clear that certain patterns of choice do exist. Site locations were not randomly selected.

Researchers as varied as physicists and psychics are just beginning to recognize that some regions of the earth's crust appear to have enhanced levels of radiation and electromagnetism in their midst. In fact, a good many mysterious places are characterized by magnetic and electrical anomalies and even measurable variations in gravity perhaps caused by geological fault zones deep within the earth. It's been suggested that these places somehow influence people's behavior or consciousness. Perhaps this is the "positive" and "negative" energy paradigm referred to earlier. What is intriguing, however, is the apparent harmonious link between geology and human existence. Perhaps rocks *do* affect us in ways that were fully appreciated in ancient times, when people were not cut off from the land by steel and glass buildings webbed with their own electromagnetic fields. If there is any truth to this, it would be crucial to understand the biological mechanisms involved.

Upper Cataract Creek, near the Grand Canyon, Arizona. (Reprinted from Winchell, Sketches of Creation)

Geological Overview

Almost everywhere in the Rocky Mountain West, solid rock forms the skeleton of the landscape, the framework upon which the delicate skin of the cultural scene has been molded. Yet this apparent immobility is an illusion. The landscape is dynamic and has been since its inception. In the past million years the earth has experienced at least ten ice ages. During the last glaciation, huge sheets of ice, some more than two miles thick, spread across North America. Because a great deal of the ocean was locked up in glaciers, sea levels dropped and exposed vast tracts of ocean floor. The previously submerged continental shelves connected the hemispheres, making Asia, America, Europe, and Africa a single gigantic land mass.

Glaciers had a savage effect on America. Some thirty thousand years ago, drastic changes in the earth's climate brought Arctic weather to the Rocky Mountains. An ice sheet thousands of feet thick crept southward across the North American continent. Bedrock was scraped, gouged, and carried off by the advancing ice. Each year, layers of unmelted snow hardened and added further weight to the glaciers. Ice eventually covered most of the Great Plains

Fig. 1.1. Cathy Bookey points to bedrock gouged by glacial boulders twelve thousand years ago.

before stopping its southward advance. Although it has been over thirteen thousand years since the end of the last ice age, the effects of that epoch are still relatively clear (see Figure 1.1).

Not all glaciers melted uniformly when the earth's temperature increased. As the partly frozen sheets retreated northward, massive chunks of ice broke off and lay isolated, strewn about on bedrock much like soil-filled ice cubes scattered across a patio floor. Glacial debris, often consisting of large boulders known as *erratics*, was deposited over vast areas when the stagnant ice melted. Rocks formerly encrusted within the ice sheet fell free, smashing into one another and creating perfect conditions in the ensuing centuries for rapid soil formation. Steep-sided hills of stratified sand and gravel, known as *glacial kames*, were formed while potholes in the glaciers filled up with debris. Large clusters of glacial ice trapped in the upper reaches of mountains eroded the sides of these peaks into bowl-shaped depressions known as *cirques*.

Glacial ice did melt quite rapidly, however. Heavy rains coupled with increasing amounts of meltwater transported large volumes of soil and rock into lowland regions. The abrasive action of weathering wore down many soft sharp-edged stones into gravel, while hard boulders composed of granite and gneiss often survive into the present. Boulders tumbled and slid down hillsides, and larger erratics deposited on cliff tops remained in place, undisturbed for centuries.

Throughout the millennia, wind, water, and the destructive effects of repeated freezing and thawing removed much of the base soil under many

Fig. 1.2. Midnineteenth-century Americans frolicking atop a glacial erratic. (Reprinted from Harper's Weekly)

glacially deposited erratics. Erosion left only the more resistant rocks underneath the boulders. Thus, perched rocks are very commonly found in areas of past glacial activity, such as in Rocky Mountain National Park; they are features that many native groups regarded as sacred and that early white settlers disregarded as meaningless. In fact, quite a number of these structures were probably pushed over cliffsides by good-humored explorers and pioneers (see Figure 1.2). But, as geological writer Jerome Wyckoff has stated, "Enough oddly placed rocks remain...to prompt some people to say 'now who could have done that?'"[1]

There are many geological anomalies in the Rocky Mountain West (see Figure 1.3). Some predate the glacial era. Others are the result of the glacial meltdown. Some are massive geoforms, while others are as small as pebbles. Details about these strange structures follow the Archeological Overview.

Archeological Overview

Almost twenty thousand years ago, nomadic bands of big-game hunters trekked across the Bering land bridge from Siberia to Alaska. Successive migrations of these ancient Asians moved into a strange and wild countryside. There they slaughtered unsuspecting herds of woolly elephants, giant sloths, and big horn elk. Each year the animal supply dwindled as a consequence of overkill, and hunters were obliged to push farther and farther south in search of new game.

Around ten thousand years ago, when the great ice masses finally melted and released billions of gallons of trapped water into the world's oceans, the bridge from Asia to America was covered up. The newly formed Bering Strait isolated the continent from further land migrations. Groups of hunters remaining in the Western Hemisphere spread into widely divergent climates as the last uncomfortable stages of the ice age trickled to a halt. In a few centuries, then, the entire Western Hemisphere from Alaska to the southern tip of America was traversed and occupied by people who much later in time would erroneously be called "Indians."

When Christopher Columbus sailed into the Caribbean, more than one hundred centuries had passed since the last ice age. What had happened in the interval between the last glacial stream and 1492? Were both North and South America unknown to the rest of the world for over ten thousand years?

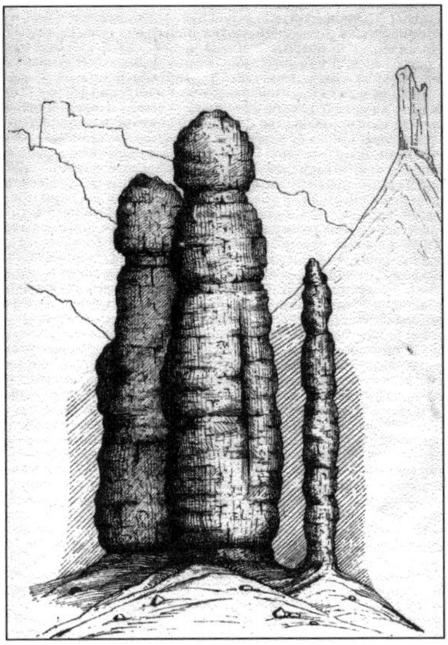

Ancient Visitors?

There is an ongoing controversy between professional archeologists and well-meaning amateur researchers about the possibility that Native Americans were visited and their culture influenced by prehistoric Old World explorers. Briefly put, amateur researchers claim their proof consists of scriptlike markings found on pebbles, boulders, in caves, and on cliffsides throughout America. The markings are said to resemble various ancient Old World writing systems (see Figure 1.4).

Fig. 1.3. *Monuments in White River Canyon.* (Reprinted from Hayden, *Tenth Annual Report,* author's collection)

Professional archeologists discount these claims, saying the markings are either tool scratchings or some other Indian-based tallying system. They ask the amateurs: Where are the burial sites, the garbage pits, the homes of these hypothetical Old World explorers? Good question. The amateurs respond: They haven't been found yet! Perhaps.

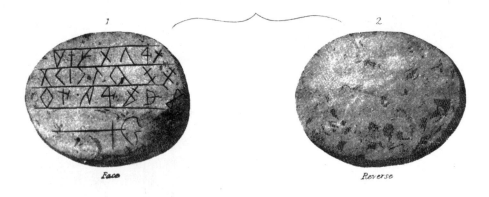

Fig. 1.4. Inscribed stone found in an ancient earthen burial mound at Grave Creek, West Virginia, in the 1800s. (Reprinted from Schoolcraft, History of the Indian Tribes of the United States, author's collection)

The antagonism between these two groups is visceral, and great fun to watch in action. Some of the archeological sites listed in this book have mutually exclusive or multiple explanations—it all depends on which group you listen to. This guide will merely list the sites and the differing viewpoints, when available. But first, to fully understand the nature of the disagreement, some historical perspective is needed.

When the pragmatic pioneers pushed into the wilderness felling trees and clearing fields, they incidentally noticed buried stone chambers, monstrous boulders balanced on smaller rocks, massive earthen mounds, and other stone ruins (see Figures 1.5, 1.6, and 1.7).

They didn't dwell on the matter too long, though, for they were busy scratching out an existence in a frightening and hostile country. Distinguished savants of the time, however, observing the chaotic, and what they thought to be barbaric, customs of the native population, reasoned that a different people must have erected the curious field stones. The "savages" weren't capable of such feats, they thought.

An examination of early records and trail guides yields enticing accounts. For example, Captain John Smith in his description of Virginia mentions that

Fig. 1.5. The Great Mound, near Miamisburg, Ohio, is typical of the mysteries encountered by the early settlers of America. (Reprinted from Baldwin, *Ancient America in Notes on American Archaeology*, author's collection)

Fig. 1.6. Inexplicable earthworks at Hopeton, Ohio. Combinations of the square and circle are common in these ancient works. So perfect were the figures that an early team of investigators remarked, "the builders possessed a standard of measurement, and had a means of determining angles." (Reprinted from Baldwin, *Ancient America*)

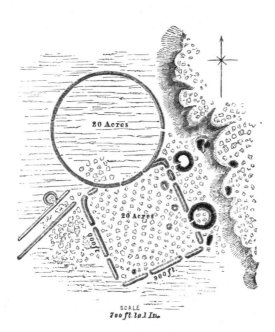

Fig. 1.7. Plan survey of the Hopeton earthworks. (Reprinted from Baldwin, *Ancient America*)

Fig. 1.8. Standing stones in southwestern Colorado. (Reprinted from Hayden, *Tenth Annual Report*)

many Indians had "altar stones" scattered throughout the wilderness; most were erected to offer sacrifices upon after a return from war, hunting trips, or at other special occasions. Among the Blackfoot Indians of northwest Canada, says an early encyclopedia, were sacred standing stones as well as sacrificial altar stones. Human blood was smeared on them in honor of a god. Some were also rubbed against as a cure for barrenness (see Figures 1.8 and 1.9).

Circles of stones were described in an 1824 issue of the *American Journal of Science*. A geologist reported that a stone circle on a high hill outside the town of Hudson, New York, attracted attention "many years ago on account of the remarkable size of the stones, and their position."[2] The same geologist cited another account of stones he was sure had been placed by ancient peoples. Termed "Sacrifice Rocks," they were said to be on the side of the road between the towns of Plymouth and Sandwich in Massachusetts. Standing between four and six feet high, they were frequently visited by Indians who made numerous offerings there.

Henriette Mertz, a Chicago attorney who has written extensively about ancient sailing routes to America, uncovered some impressive reports of early pioneers in the Pennsylvania State Archives. In one of her books she wrote:

Fig. 1.9. A standing stone in northwestern Massachusetts. The owners of the property on which this stone stands have historical documents indicating the stone was in place at the time their ancestors purchased the land, in the 1700s.

When modern man pushed into the interior from Chesapeake Bay sometime late in the seventeenth century and up the Susquehanna beyond Harrisburg, two important markers had been discovered—one standing near the old site of Frank's Town and the other just beyond Huntingdon, marking the proper fork of the river at the confluence. Huntingdon stands today on a site which in Revolutionary War times was known as Standing Stone. Here at this spot an ancient stone marker once towered on a promontory. Amazed explorers described the stone as an obelisk—fourteen feet high, broad of base, tapering to six or seven inches at the top, covered on all four sides with indecipherable letters, believed by some who first saw it to have been Egyptian hieroglyphics. This stone has frequently been mentioned in Pennsylvania archives—the original disappeared about 1755. This is only one of a great many recorded standing stones that the earliest travelers and explorers found marking the trail from the Atlantic to the Ohio by water—a trail of standing stone markers found as far west as Lancaster, Ohio.[3]

In the early 1800s, after the initial problems of settlement had been worked out, scholars began roaming America in search of something to study. Fur trappers and settlers had reported the existence of earthen ruins and stone debris, and naturalists and geologists were telling the same stories. Based on the findings, many assumed quite matter-of-factly that an extinct, non-Indian civilization had inhabited early America. Books and lectures of a hypothetical ancient race sparked public imagination for decades. The title of an 1853 best seller by William Pidgeon,

Top: *Fig. 1.10. A skeleton uncovered from stone grave, Fort Ancient, Ohio, in the late 1800s.* (Reprinted from Baldwin, *Ancient America*)

Right: *Fig. 1.11. An 1870 map of stone ruins in the eastern U.S.* (Reprinted from Peet, *The Mound Builders: Their Works and Relics*, author's collection)

Bottom: *Fig. 1.12. This fanciful image of an imaginary battle between the so-called ancient American race and Native Americans fostered a decidedly negative attitude toward indigenous Americans, proclaiming as it did that Native tribes wiped out the "superior" mound-building race sometime in prehistory.* (Reprinted from Pidgeon, *Traditions of Dee-coo-dah and Antiquarian Researches*, author's collection)

Fig 1.13. Stone-lined graves in Tennessee, excavated in the 1870s by the Smithsonian team. (From Powell, *Ninth Annual Report*, author's collection)

a fur trader and explorer, pretty much sums up the attitude of the period: *Traditions of Dee-Coo-Dah and Antiquarian Researchers: Comprising Extensive Explorations, Surveys, and Excavations of the Wonderful and Mysterious Earthen Remains of the Mound Builders in America; the Traditions of the Last Prophet of the Elk Nation Relative to Their Origin and Use; and the Evidence of an Ancient Population More Numerous Than the Present Aborigines.* (See Figures 1.10, 1.11, 1.12, and 1.13.)

On Isle Royale National Park in Lake Superior, and in northern Michigan, thousands of worked copper mines were discovered as early as the sixteenth century by French Jesuit missionaries, who reported that the Indians of the peninsula knew absolutely nothing about their origins. In 1849, Dr. Charles T. Jackson, in his geological report to the United States government, gave the first systematic description of the upper Michigan-Wisconsin mining works. Of one mine approximately thirty feet in depth, Dr. Jackson wrote: "...not far below the bottom of a trough-like cavity, among a mass of leaves, sticks, and water [lay] a detached mass of copper weighing nearly six tons. It lay upon a cob-work of round logs or skids six or eight inches in diameter, the ends of which showed plainly the marks of a small axe or cutting tool about two and a half inches wide. They soon shriveled and decayed when exposed to the air. The mass of copper had been raised several feet, along the foot of the lode, on timbers, by means of wedges."[4]

Within the trench was a thirty-five-pound stone maul and a twenty-five-pound copper sledge. "Old trees showing 395 rings of annual growth stood in the debris, and the fallen and decayed trunks of trees of a former generation were seen lying across the pits."[5] (See Figures 1.14 and 1.15.)

Jackson went on to detail another remarkable mining site. In the face of a vertical bluff, some ancient people had dug a shaft twenty-five feet in length, fifteen feet high, and twelve feet deep. He reported that some of the stone blocks removed from the recess must have weighed two to three tons, and required some type of lever to get them out. Once the surface rubbish was cleared away, Dr. Jackson found the remains of a gutter or trough made of cedar, placed to carry water away from the mine. At the bottom of the excavation a piece of white cedar timber was found on which were the marks of an axe. Cedar shovels, mauls, copper gads or wedges, charcoal, and ashes were discovered, over which "primeval" forest trees had grown to full size.[6]

Although nineteenth-century scholars were totally perplexed by these mines, it was evident that they were all dug by a common people a very long time ago. The mines were said to show the same methods of excavation, the

Fig. 1.15. Copper ore from the upper Michigan peninsula.

Fig. 1.14. Diagram
of an ancient
copper-mining shaft,
Isle Royale National
Park, Lake Superior
(a, mass of copper;
b, bottom of shaft;
c, earth and debris
excavated from
mine). The dark
spots below b are
masses of copper yet
to be extracted.
(Reprinted from
Baldwin, Ancient
America)

same implements, the same peculiarities both of knowledge and lack of knowledge, and the same amount of debris and growth covering up the openings. But the scientists of the last century were at a loss to identify the "common people" who dug the shafts. In fact, after one hundred years of investigation, the deep tunnels and gaping storage pits of Michigan and Wisconsin remain an intriguing archeological mystery.

Recent carbon-14 dating of organic matter taken from the shafts dates them to well over three thousand years ago. Furthermore, metallurgical engineers estimate that more than a billion pounds of copper were mined out of this region: to date, this amount of mined copper has not been found in the United States! Author Henriette Mertz, who also has extensively studied this mystery, once wrote: "This incredible amount of copper has not been accounted for by American archeologists—the sum total according to archeological findings here in the states amounts to a mere handful of copper beads and trinkets—float copper. Five hundred thousand tons of pure copper does not disintegrate into thin air—it cannot be sneezed away—it must be somewhere...[7]

But where?

By the late nineteenth century, in response to a popular literature claiming that just about everyone from Noah and his ark to Caesar and his legions had stormed across America, the Smithsonian Institution began its first systematic exploration of this country's earthen heaps. It gave Professor Cyrus Thomas five thousand dollars and three field workers to compile "the most definitive and comprehensive report to date" on the mounds. While Thomas spent a good deal of his time in Washington coordinating the attack, his assistants routinely prodded, dug, and contaminated over two thousand mounds in the states of Alabama, Arkansas, Florida, Georgia, Illinois, Iowa, Kentucky, Louisiana, Michigan, Minnesota, Mississippi, Missouri, New York, North Dakota, North Carolina, Ohio, Pennsylvania, South Carolina, South Dakota, Tennessee, Wisconsin, and West Virginia (see Figure 1.16).

The field team was not looking for anything special: it was simply interested in recording the major contents of each structure and sending the report to Washington. Thomas faithfully relied upon his diggers' reports for a good many of the gutted earthworks. He concluded, among other things, that "nothing found in the mounds justifies the opinion that they are uniformly of great antiquity," and that "the links of evidence connecting the Indians and mound-builders are so numerous and well established as to justify archeologists in assuming that they were one and the same people."

In 1894, the Smithsonian issued the *Twelfth Annual Report of the Bureau*

Fig. 1.16. This map shows the distribution of mounds gutted by Cyrus Thomas's field workers on behalf of the Smithsonian Institution in the late 1890s. (Reprinted from Powell, Twelfth Annual Report, *author's collection)*

of Ethnology to the Secretary of the Smithsonian Institution, which flatly denied, based on Thomas's work, that any evidence existed for a non-Indian people visiting America before the fifteenth-century discovery by Columbus. The framework of the report eventually became the official doctrine and dogma behind American archeological thinking. A rigid scientific paradigm was thus

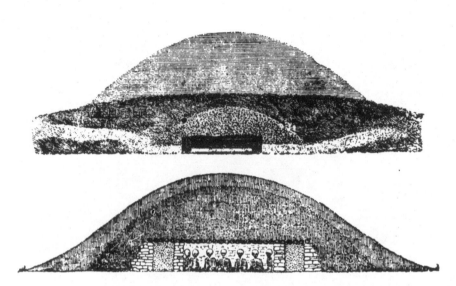

Fig. 1.17. Top: *This section of a Bronze Age grave from northern Europe shows the ground level, with its arrangement of stones, cists, and mound.* Bottom: *Section of a mound from East Dubuque, Illinois, excavated in the 1800s. The similarity of this burial chamber to those of the European mounds convinced American researchers of a cultural connection.* (Reprinted from Peet, *The Mound Builders*)

established. Although many universities in the early twentieth century had ample opportunity to examine potential sites, after the report most archeology departments cautiously ignored the American enigmas and concentrated on more exotic lands like Egypt and the Middle East. Work on the earthworks was considered taboo for many professionals. And local ordinances in mound-building counties frequently restricted further excavation and destruction of the sites.

By the early 1930s, however, various people began to advance theories designed to bring substance to this intellectual vacuum. The usual crop of ancient peoples was listed on America's guest list: the Jews, the Phoenicians, the Carthaginians, the Greeks, the Scythians, the Chinese, the Swedes, the Welsh, and the Celts. Although a few theories offered a starting point for scientific scrutiny, many of the ideas created real difficulties. The problem lay in the way the arguments were presented. Authors accepted certain assumptions as true and then built their respective cases around them. In their earnest efforts to prove their theories, they played a Rorschach game, projecting their

Fig. 1.18. A mid-nineteenth-century engraving of the Newport Tower, Newport, Rhode Island. In 1839, based on supposed architectural similarities specific to medieval buildings, the Danish scholar C. A. Rafn claimed the structure was an eleventh- or twelfth-century Norse church. For many years after this, the tower was believed to be the definitive construction proving pre-Columbian European contact with America. The heated controversy that arose in the academic community prompted officials of Harvard's Peabody Museum to sponsor a full-scale archeological dig at the site from 1948 through 1949. The careful digging proved that the tower was built no earlier than the seventeenth century. And, because Newport was founded in 1639 as a seaport, the revised interpretation of the tower suggested it was built as a "look-out tower" for seagoing vessels. The very fact that disagreement over the tower's origins raged for many years after it was constructed shows how much information about America's origins has been lost in only three hundred years! Recent work by Copenhagen scientists who have dated the mortar between the lower stones places the date of construction to the late sixteenth or early seventeenth century. But the mystery continues. If the tower was constructed by English settlers, the English foot, the standard unit of measurement in England at the time, would have been used in the tower. It wasn't. In fact, the only standard measurement discovered in the tower's construction was one used in southern Europe. A team of scientists from the New England–based Early Sites Research Society has recently completed the first phase of a magnetic ground scan around the tower. Intriguingly, there are many "subsurface features"—underground disturbances—in and around the structure. The mystery continues… (Reprinted from Baldwin, Ancient America)

pet ideas into ancient legends, scripts, and artifacts. The unfortunate part was that the unknowing public readily accepted such flotsam as established dogma. Myth was elevated into fact. (See Figures 1.17 and 1.18.)

Given the almost carnival atmosphere surrounding the study of America's dim past (outside the realm of the Native Americans), very few reputable archeologists and historians in the 1940s and 1950s dared tread on such academically dangerous ground. The feeling has endured even into the present.

Throughout the 1960s, 1970s, and into the 1980s, several writers and pseudoscientists suggested that dozens of prehistoric ethnic groups had all sailed to and settled in America, leaving strange mysteries in their wake. But the facts were speculative and the arguments weak. Various publications made it a point to outdo one another by presenting wild and exotic ideas about these "facts." Theories are easy to come by, and authors were quick to fantasize on a kaleidoscope of new and old topics (see Figure 1.19). Thus, the Americas were visited by spacemen in god drag, misplaced monks in junks, adventurous Arabs, and wandering Israelites. Most of these accounts read like so much pastry for the brain, and they are partially responsible for

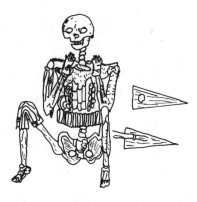

Fig. 1.19. A tracing of a nineteenth-century engraving of a severely decomposed body discovered in 1831 near Fall River, Massachusetts. A corroded brass breastplate, some brass tubes, and arrowheads were found with the corpse. Its discovery caused much debate at the time. Some argued the body was of a Viking. Others claimed it was an even earlier European. Longfellow made the find famous with his romantic poem, "Skeleton in Armour." The skeleton probably was the burial of a seventeenth-century English explorer. It was destroyed in the late 1830s, when the barn in which it was stored burned down. (After Holland, *The Bay Path*)

the negative attitude of the American archeological community. The sites are open to anyone's weird explanation, and the mysteries continue.

Inscriptions

Throughout the millennia, various cultural, ecological, and geographical factors have tended to channel human thought and expression into many dif-

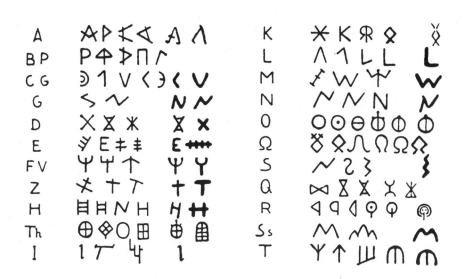

Fig. 1.20. Ancient Iberic script. (Reprinted from Fenn, *Grafica Prehistorica de Espana y El Origen de la Cultura Europea,* author's collection)

ferent types of writing schemes. The first writing systems seem to have been designed to meet the specific needs of their creators: Babylonian laundry lists abound. But in time, simple expressions took on broader, more provocative meanings. Within certain bounds, people having a written language could silently communicate with others sharing the same mode of expression. Societies were able to record their doings and pass them on to later generations. Secrets learned from the trials and errors of one age could be transmitted through time to the next. During the Bronze Age in the Mediterranean, for example, there existed hundreds of forms of script. Some alphabets continued to be used by peripheral cultures on the fringes of the Middle East, northwestern Spain, and Ireland, while others passed into disuse and oblivion.

Interest in ancient languages began with the explorations of the fifteenth, sixteenth, and seventeenth centuries, which fostered a new sense of antiquity throughout the Old World. Travelers returned home with fantastic stories about strange inscriptions from such countries as Egypt, Greece, and the Americas. Speculations about these exotic markings were at first fanciful and then mystical. But these explanations had no place in late eighteenth-century Europe, when scholars began to codify and classify the mass of curios collected from diverse regions of the globe. A critical, comparative method was emerging. It was during this time that the so-called great age of decipherment had its beginnings.

Epigraphy, or the study of inscriptions (particularly ancient ones), is a sociological phenomenon specific to the modern world. As Oxford University Professor Maurice Pope has noted, only in the last two or three centuries have people set out to recover the key to "lost" writing systems.

As one might suspect, there are a host of technical terms and definitions specific to epigraphic analysis. For our purposes it is unnecessary to detail all of these items, but there are a few that should be clarified. The term *script* refers to a total writing system, complete with its punctuation, special symbols, and different phonetic values. A script is usually made up of an *alphabet*, which is a set of letters, each having a particular way of being pronounced. A *language*, in contrast, is the method of communication used between a people. To decipher means to explain the individual signs of a script. It does not mean understanding the message expressed by it. In the words of Professor Pope: "Decipherment opens the gate, interpretation passes into the field beyond." [8]

The people with whose inscriptions we are most familiar range from those who settled Europe to those who settled North Africa. The fate of the lands in the western Mediterranean was essentially determined by these settlers, who came from the sea. As early as five thousand years ago, Neolithic tribes sailed along the Atlantic seacoast and built massive stone monuments. [9] The Iberian Peninsula (modern Portugal and Spain) was subject to several waves of immigrant peoples. The peninsula natives, appropriately known as Iberians, suffered the onslaught of Celtic tribes that swept through the Pyrenees from the east. Under the brutal discipline of these hordes, a new form of culture took root. A curious blending of Celtic and Iberian art stonework known as Celt-Iberian developed and flourished. Powerful trading outposts, such as the Kingdom of Tartessos in the southwestern part of the peninsula, maintained strong economic ties through gold and copper with merchant Phoenicians. About the same time, groups of Libyans from the North African coast sailed to Iberia's fertile Andalusian plains and began to lay the foundations of an intensive agricultural system in southern Spain.

Thus by the late Bronze Age (3,500 to 4,000 years ago), a variety of "foreign peoples" were mingling with the native Iberians: Celts, Libyans, and Phoenician- Carthaginians. According to the late Harvard University Professor Barry Fell, the writing systems these groups supposedly brought with them underwent dialectic changes when they came in contact with the native Iberian language.

Mediterranean scholars have long puzzled over Iberic script (see Figure 1.20). Although it was deciphered over fifty years ago, no one could read the language until 1975, when Dr. Fell first claimed he had worked out the script—curiously enough, from American examples on Susquehanna field stones—by reading it as Basque.[10] Fell then examined inscriptions from Spain and argued that he was able to differentiate between native Iberic script and script that had been written by the Libyans living there. Moreover, this writing system was found to be a Libyan dialect of the Carthaginian Punic language. It appeared further that some ancient scribes wrote this "Iberian Punic," as Dr. Fell called it, in the alphabet of the early Basques (Iberic script), while

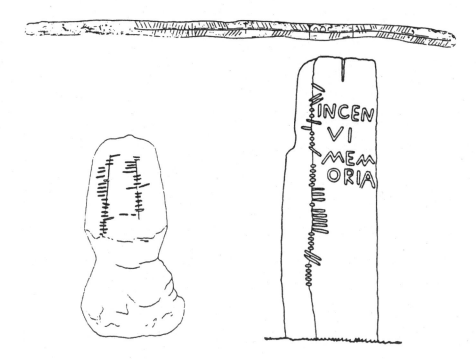

Fig. 1.21. Top: *a side view of the famed Bressay Stone from Scotland, showing Ogam script markings. On the face of this slab is an intricate series of bas-relief Celtic carvings.* (Reprinted from Wilson, *Prehistoric Annals of Scotland,* author's collection) Left: *Ogam stone from Silchester, England, circa A.D. 300.* Right: *Ogam stone from Lewannick, Cornwall, England, circa A.D. 300.* (Reprinted from Horsford, *An Inscribed Stone,* author's collection)

others wrote it in the more familiar Semitic alphabet of the early Greeks.

But Fell didn't stop there. He also said that the many Celt-Iberian inscriptions, which had also baffled Spanish scholars for centuries, were in fact Iberian versions of what would later become known as *Goidelic Celtic*, the language of the Celtic peoples of Ireland and the Scottish Highlands (to be distinguished from the pre-Saxon *Brythonic* Celts of Brittany, Wales, and England, who spoke a different tongue).[11] The Celt-Iberian research also suggested a totally revolutionary theory: that the Celtic alphabet, known as *Ogam*, originated in Iberia around 800 B.C. and then spread north to Ireland (see Figure 1.21). The orthodox view is that the Irish in the fourth century A.D. invented it and used it for simple mnemonics or gravestone inscriptions.

With only one exception, letters of the Ogam alphabet were represented by straight lines that derived their significance from their position on a continuous horizontal or vertical line. The Celt-Iberian alphabet differed from the British Ogam in that it was without vowels, but, other than a few differences in consonants, the alphabet, according to Fell, appeared on stones in stylistically the same manner as did the Irish Ogam of the fourth century. In summary, Fell believed:

> 1. That he had partially "cracked the code" of Iberic inscriptions from northern Portugal and Spain on the basis of suspected Iberic inscriptions found in America.
>
> 2. That in ancient Iberia the Punic language was written with native Iberic letters like those used in inscriptions found in America.
>
> 3. That a hitherto unrecognized form of alphabet called *Celt-Iberian Ogam* had simultaneously come to light in the western Mediterranean and North America.

The discovery of inscribed stones in the United States has had a long and embittered history marred by forgeries, professional tirades, blind ambition, cover-ups, and academic tiptoeing. Hundreds of tablets with various types of markings have been reported since Colonial days (see Figure 1.22), but for one reason or another—the conditions under which the inscriptions were found, for instance, or their inaccessibility after discovery—most were simply ignored. Scholars accepting the established scenario of an isolated American continent could consider only two possibilities for stones etched with an ancient European script: Either they were forgeries, or they were authentic but had been brought to America and planted in modern times. The framework of scientific thought allowed no other conclusions.

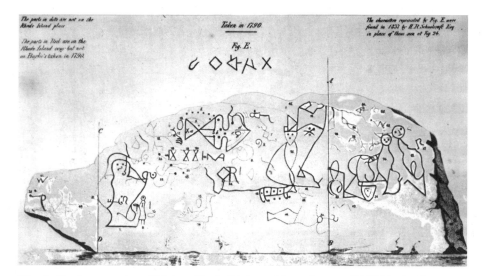

Fig. 1.22. An engraving of Dighton Rock, Dighton, Massachusetts. In 1712, the Puritan clergyman Cotton Mather first reported this inscribed boulder in Transactions of the Royal Society, *London. Years later, the rock, then situated a short distance inland from the Taunton River at the head of Assonet Bay, attracted much attention due to its supposed ancient Scandinavian origin. The noted American historian Henry Rowe Schoolcraft sketched the site in 1837 and, with the aid of a Native American interpreter, concluded that the markings represented an "Algonquin pictographic record of an Indian battle." William Pidgeon revived national interest in the rock when, in 1858, he proclaimed (on very shaky ground!) to have seen "Phoenician letters legibly engraved" on its surface. By the turn of the century, scholars rightly dismissed Pidgeon's interpretation as nonsense. Today, most authorities believe the inscription is of Native origin. (Reprinted from Schoolcraft,* History of the Indian Tribes)

In recent years, other explanations have been offered to account for hundreds of so-called marked stones. Archeologists have dismissed the markings as by-products of natural erosion, impressions of growing tree roots, scratches from field plows, impressions from the sharpening of stone tools, or as undocumented Indian tally-mark systems.

That some inscriptions have been faked is undeniable. The motivations of the forgers were many: some sought to confuse the historical record and subsequently ruin the careers of their naive colleagues, while others deceived early museums and universities merely for profit or thrills. Bad publicity associated with bogus stones has tended to enhance the doubts of the academic community. But most of these fake stones are unique in quality, and this singularity is the key element that makes them suspect. Furthermore, as the noted Semiticist Dr. Cyrus Gordon acidly remarked in his book, *Riddles in History*, to doubt the authenticity of the multitude of inscriptions brought to light in the Western Hemisphere, "it has become necessary to demonstrate a plot stretching at least from 1872 to 1971. A ring of forgers or pranksters must be shown to have operated in Brazil, Minnesota, Maine, and Europe."[12]

One might still ask, Have there ever been any ancient inscriptions found lying next to, or in close association with, an established archeological site? An engraving of an inscribed tablet excavated from a burial mound at Bat Creek, Tennessee, by Cyrus Thomas was published in the 1894 volume of the *Twelfth Annual Report to the Secretary of the Smithsonian*. The circumstances of the find suggested that there was no intrusion after burial. That is, once the mound was sealed, it wasn't opened up again until Thomas arrived on the scene. The symbols on the stone were abruptly dismissed in the report as "beyond question, letters of the Cherokee alphabet." Cherokee was a syllabary devised in 1821 by an Indian chief after his return from England. The characters consisted of eighty-five inverted and transformed Roman letters com-

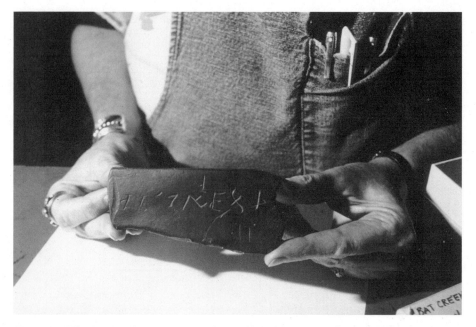

Fig. 1.23. The Bat Creek Stone, oriented as published by the Smithsonian in 1894. The stone is stored in a box in the basement of the Smithsonian Institution.

bined with some European numerals and a few arbitrary characters (see Figure 1.23).

The matter rested there until 1964, when, seventy years after the Smithsonian report was published, Henriette Mertz pointed out that the Smithsonian Institution had mistakenly published the engraving of the stone upside down. When Ms. Mertz simply turned the illustration around, the Semitic characters etched onto the artifact became strikingly obvious (see Figure 1.24). Cyrus Gordon, who later investigated the stone, concluded that the inscription had been carved in a style of Hebraic script that was used in the Middle East around A.D. 100![13]

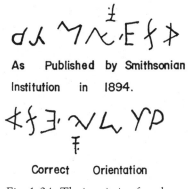

As Published by Smithsonian Institution in 1894.

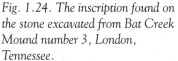

Correct Orientation

Fig. 1.24. The inscription found on the stone excavated from Bat Creek Mound number 3, London, Tennessee.

At Grave Creek, West Virginia, in 1838, another inscribed tablet was found at the bottom of a sixty-foot mound. Henry Schoolcraft, a distinguished nineteenth-century historian, mentioned it in his voluminous work on the American Indian: "This curious relic...appears to reveal, in the unknown past, evidences of European intrusion into the continent."[14] Copies of the inscription were sent to several European scholars. Most of them dismissed it as nonsense. Professor Rafn of Copenhagen, however, declared quite confidently that the markings were Celt-Iberic.

In the New World there are mysterious markings on rocks that may tell a story spanning millennia. The issue is *what* and *whose* story is it? (See Figures 1.25 and 1.26.)

Alignments

The orientation of many ruined structures and caves in the Rocky Mountains appear to be aligned toward key solar horizon spots—areas where the sun sets or rises on specific dates. Many sites give the distinct impression of being the aged and ruined vestiges of an ancient solar calendar system.

In the course of twelve months, the sun moves across the horizon on a methodical journey (see Figure 1.27). On the first days of spring and of autumn, known respectively as the *vernal equinox* (March 21) and the *autumnal equinox* (September 21), the sun rises due east and sets due west, and day and night are everywhere of equal length. As summer approaches, sunrise moves

Fig. 1.25. Carved hands on a rock wall in the Purgatoire River Valley of southeastern Colorado. Student researcher Margaret Hoover lends scale to the carvings.

Fig. 1.26. Inscribed rock panel from southeastern Colorado. Student researcher Anna Cayton-Holland points to a gridlike section of pecked dots near the top of the photo. Note the line with vertical slashes underneath it near the left side of the photo.

farther north each day until late June, when it appears to slow, stop, and begin moving southward again. June 21, the day its northward motion stops, is the *summer solstice*. Half a year later, the *winter solstice*, December 21, signals the end of its southward movement along the horizon. The solstices are unique moments of the year. As soon as two or more sticks or stones are placed in the ground, a visual vantage point is created from which the sun's movement across the sky can be observed. The

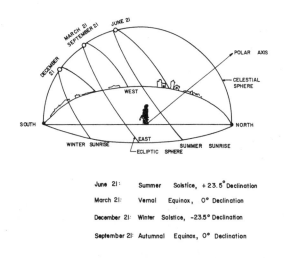

June 21:   Summer   Solstice, + 23.5° Declination

March 21:   Vernal   Equinox,   0° Declination

December 21: Winter Solstice, –23.5° Declination

September 21: Autumnal Equinox, 0° Declination

Fig. 1.27. The sun's daily path through the seasons.

beauty of such an event becomes acute as each season's sunlight shifts shadows, changing the tone and character of a land. But the act of marking out the sun's path is not only aesthetic, it is functional as well. The two solstices, once plotted out via some permanent marker, become reference points for devising a solar calendar.

Throughout the American West there are reports depicting similar arrangements of placed stones. There are stones protruding out of the ground in clear view of the equinox sunrises and sunsets, perched rocks lying in conjunction with stone semicircles on high bluffs above waterways, and cracks in caves that allow sunlight to enter on the solstices.

The discovery and appreciation of geological and archeological anomalies is habit-forming. People are starting to notice stone mysteries that prior generations passed by with indifference. Perhaps changing demographic and social patterns are contributing to this renewed interest in the past. Perhaps it is part of America's search for its origins. In either case it is clear that *noticing* an anomaly reflects the ever-changing Zeitgeist.

The mysterious sites to follow will give the field explorer much to contemplate.

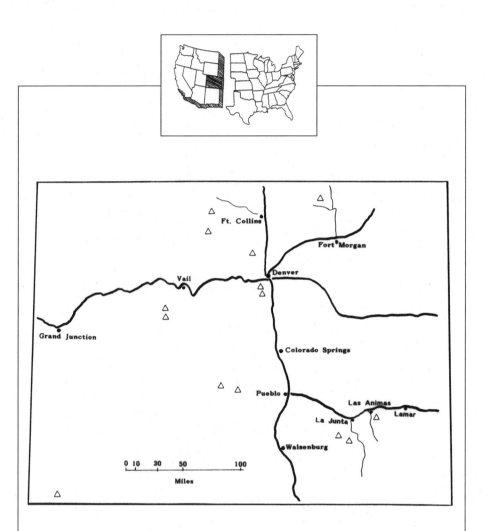

Mysterious Sites in Colorado

2

Colorado

Colorado is the starting point on our journey to mysterious places. There are a multitude of sites scattered throughout this state with scenery that "bankrupts the English language," as former president Theodore Roosevelt once put it.

Colorado is a state of dreams. Fifteen thousand years ago the first nomadic hunters scoured the terrain in search of large animals. They were probably following a vision quest into an unknown region filled with a multitude of food. Projectile points dating to that period found in the mountains and plains of Colorado suggest that migratory bands of these big-game hunters made repeated seasonal treks. Much later in time Anasazi Indians built cliff dwellings along the southern corridor of the state. Their mysterious ruins punctuate a large part of Colorado's southwestern fringe. Along the Apishapa and Purgatoire River valleys in the southeast, another ancient Indian group built strange stone circles hundreds of feet above the riverbed.

In 1540, Spanish conquistador Francisco Coronado and others wandered through the central plains of the region in search of a golden dream: the Seven Cities of Cibola—the fabled cities of gold. They failed to find the imaginary cities. In the mid-1800s gold *was* found at the confluence of two rivers near the north-central part of the territory, and the rush was on. The city of Denver was established as a supply center. A few years later, when gold was uncovered in the canyons along the clear mountain creeks west of Denver, the rush to Colorado was firmly established. In a short while the territory entered statehood.

Central/Northeastern Colorado

The central part of Colorado is the most populous region of the state. Just east of the spine of the Rocky Mountains are the metropolitan areas of Fort Collins, Boulder, Denver, Colorado Springs, and Pueblo, with many smaller towns in between. Interstate highways run north to south and east to west, connecting the mountains to the grasslands.

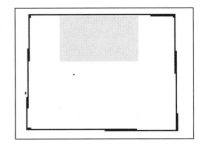

It wasn't always this way. An 1874 map of the eastern base of the Rocky Mountains lists Denver as a mere railroad "junction" (see Figure 2.1). Denver made its fortune as a supply center for the burgeoning gold-mining industry. Today the metropolitan area around Denver is home to over two million people.

Northeast and east of Denver is the high-country prairie. The land today is made up of large stretches of irrigated farms and cattle ranches. At one time buffalo stormed across this region in massive herds, and prehistoric Indian hunters followed in pursuit.

STONE SPHERE
Dinosaur Ridge, Morrison, Colorado

Site Synopsis

On a road-cut some twenty miles west of Denver, near the foothills of the Rocky Mountains, a spherical sandlike stone four-feet in diameter lies embedded in a cavity of 150-million-year-old sandstone. It first came to view when road builders in the 1930s blasted through the ridge. Several other circular cavities were found nearby. Experienced geologists cannot agree upon an explanation for this strange sphere.

Location

The sphere is north of Morrison, a town about twenty miles west of Denver. From Denver, take 6th Avenue west to Interstate

70. Travel west on the interstate, exiting at the Morrison sign. Turn left (south) at the ramp's end onto Morrison Road, traveling about one mile south before reaching the well-known Red Rocks Amphitheater on the right. Bear left off Morrison Road onto Route 26, which ascends Dinosaur Ridge. Stop at the parking area just before the road-cut. The sphere is visible from the road.

Considerations

Dinosaur Ridge is on an open-access public road. There is a self-guided geological tour one can take there.

Dinosaur Ridge is a designated National Natural Landmark; therefore, it is a protected area. This means that any artifacts, resources, rocks, plants, and fossils should not be removed or damaged.

History/Background

The stone sphere resides on a ridge that became world-famous in the late 1870s. About a quarter-mile away from the sphere, dinosaurs well known to children today were first discovered during the famed nineteenth-century golden age of exploration. Finds such as brontosaurus, stegosaurus, and allosaurus along the ridge led to a rush to track and explore this 150-million-year-old fossil deposit known as the Morrison Formation.

Sixty years after the first excavations, dinosaur tracks were discovered along the eastern slope of the ridge in a rock strata close to 100 million years old. Work there

Fig. 2.1 An 1874 map of the eastern base of the Rocky Mountains.

and elsewhere along the Front Range, the area just east of the Rocky Mountains, revealed many other extensive tracks. The 100-million-year-old strata represents the shoreline of a vast inland sea that covered most of Colorado and the Midwest. From this data it is known that dinosaurs migrated for hundreds of miles, perhaps on seasonal movements, perhaps to reach mating/nesting areas, or perhaps in search of food.

The sphere lies in the 150-million-year-old Morrison strata. It's not likely to be a dinosaur egg, for the largest ones ever found are no bigger than a football. About twenty feet below the sphere, in a strata over 200 million years old, is a hollow cavity about the same size as the spherical one (see Figure 2.2). Across the road on the opposite rock-cut, in the Morrison Formation, there is another cavity of similar dimensions.

Close examination of the object reveals a layering effect, almost like an onion, along the inner cavity. Nondestructive samples of sand collected along the side and bottom inner cavity wall and along the sphere reveal some surprising results when viewed under a dissection microscope. The sands of the sphere are very fine-grained, with no particular shape, while the inner cavity enclosing the sphere shows evidence of rapid crystallization—these grains do have a regularity of shape.

One way for tiny crystals to form is when molten rock cools rather quickly. Molten rock usually accompanies volcanic action. But in the encompassing strata there is absolutely no evidence for volcanic action. The dark layers of shale *between* the strata—representing a vastly different time period—provide evidence of volcanic dust from the region's volcanoes settling to the bottom of the ocean. Yet *something* seems to have melted the rock strata and then cooled quickly, forming the cavity.

We are stuck with the question, What is the sphere? A published geology report refers to it as a "concretion." A concretion forms when surface water precipitates through the ground and deposits its collection of minerals in a region of the sandstone. But there is much disagreement over the actual mechanism of this process. Geologists aren't sure how this happens or if the stone sphere on Dinosaur Ridge is actually such a geological formation.

Nonetheless, concretions vary in size from small pelletlike ob-

Fig. 2.2. The spherical cavity below the stone sphere, situated on the upper right.

jects to great spheres (see Figures 2.3 and 2.4). In Kansas, for example, the famed Cannonball formation (a giant spherelike concretion over ten feet in diameter) dates to the same time period as
does the sphere at Dinosaur Ridge. The size of most concretions
seems to be determined by the permeability of the host strata. Recent studies suggest that patterns in the bedding planes of rocks
represent a geological phenomenon known as "self-organization."[1]
Somehow, in ways that are difficult to explain, certain rocks seem
to have a mechanism for exhibiting self-organized patterns—this

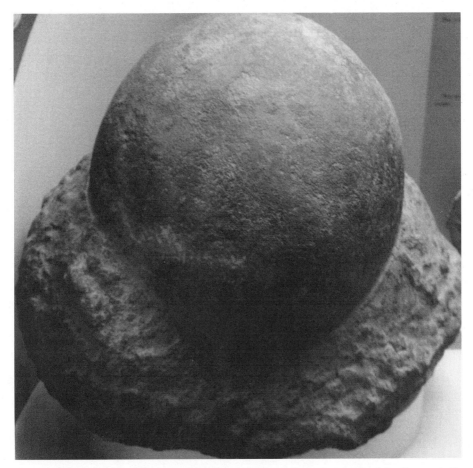

Fig. 2.3. A spherical conglomerate three feet in diameter from the mouth of the Cannonball
River in North Dakota. This specimen is now on display in the Smithsonian Institution.

includes spheres!

Although the bedding planes of a host rock pass through most concretion objects and those of the Morrison sphere do not, it is possible that the sphere is indeed a concretion deposit. A telling point is that most concretions are made of minerals that are different from the minerals of the host rock. This is true at Dinosaur Ridge.

The embedded sandstone was formed from the accumulated remains of runoff and debris. In fact, the Morrison Formation strata was at one time under the ocean. The sphere almost seems to have dropped into place and then some more sediment surrounded and covered it (note the upper layer). The same situation appears to have occurred with the other cavities noted previously. Is it possible that the sphere represents the remnants of a meteorite that smacked into the ancient sea some 150 million years ago? Could the other cavities be clues to the same cosmic phenomena? Or is it a "concretion?" The sphere at Dinosaur Ridge represents a mystery that begs explanation.

Fig. 2.4. More 100-million-year-old sandstone concretions from Oklahoma.

If permission could be obtained from the government, a core drilling through the sphere would be very revealing. Analysis of a thin tube of rock removed from the sphere could explain its origins, telling us whether it is terrestrial or not.

Contact Persons and Organizations

Morrison Natural History Museum
P.O. Box 564
Morrison, CO 80465

Colorado Geological Survey
1313 Sherman Street, Room 715
Denver, CO 80203
(303) 866-2611

Dr. Martin G. Lockley, Associate Professor of Geology
University of Colorado at Denver
Campus Box 172, P.O. Box 173364
Denver, CO 80217-3364.

SANDSTONE CUT CAVE
Hayden Green Mountain Park, northeast of Morrison, Colorado

Site Synopsis
In a sandstone ridge at the base of Green Mountain, west of Denver, is a man-made cave approximately five feet square. It extends about ten feet into the sandstone. The floor is dirt, and there is no evidence of a doorway. The purpose of this cave is unknown.

Location

From Denver, take 6th Avenue west to Interstate 70. Travel west on the interstate, exiting at the Morrison sign. Turn left (south) at the ramp's end onto Morrison Road. Travel about one

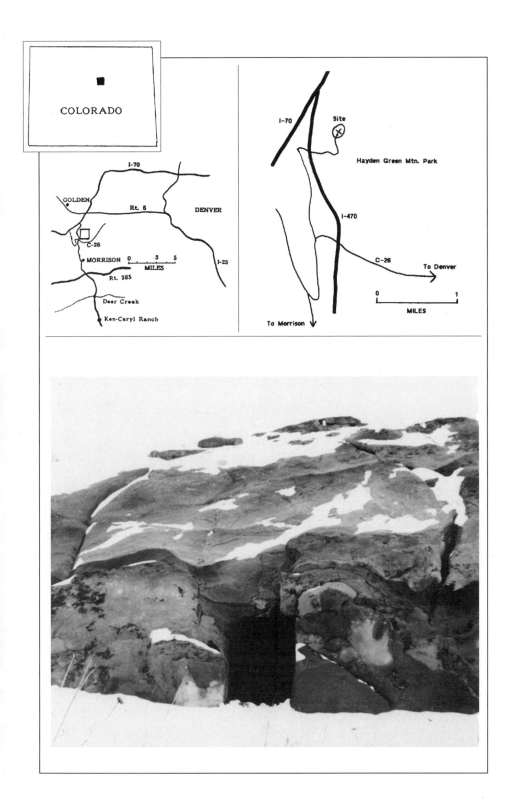

COLORADO

I-70

GOLDEN

Rt. 6

DENVER

C-26

MORRISON

0   3   5

MILES

I-25

Rt. 285

Deer Creek

Ken-Caryl Ranch

I-70

Site

Hayden Green Mtn. Park

I-470

C-26

To Denver

0   1

MILES

To Morrison

mile south before reaching the well-known Red Rocks Amphitheater, on the right. Bear left off Morrison Road onto Route 26, which ascends Dinosaur Ridge. Continue driving through the road-cut, passing the stone sphere (see page 34) on your right. Travel north along the hogback, continuing onto Rooney Road. Turn off into the Green Mountain parking area within a half-mile. From the parking area follow the trail north (within view of Route 470) for a quarter-mile. The sandstone formation is on your right.

Considerations

As with all sandstone formations, one needs to exercise care with respect to snakes. Although this park is heavily used during the summer months, one occasionally runs across reptiles and other animals. Lightweight hiking boots are recommended.

History/Background

The Colorado Historical Society's archeological division sponsored a pilot excavation a few yards from the cave site. Sometime in the mid-1800s a homesteader or miner set up a cabin behind the two "entranceway" sandstone ridges. The excavation found nails, foundation dirt, and other assorted artifacts from that period. Today, all that's left of the site is a slight mound of excavated dirt.

Because the cave is in such close proximity to the homestead site, it makes sense to link them together. Although the simple explanation suggests that the homesteaders carved the cave, the difficulty lies in its function. It's not large enough to use as an animal barn—cows don't back into tiny places, and it's much too short for a sturdy horse. As a toolshed it leaves much to be desired. The dirt floor collects water, leaving it muddy during rainy periods—winter included. No one would consider digging into sandstone for gold when gold was to be had in the mountains across the way.

What, then, is this peculiar site? It may be possible to link this cut-stone feature with a similar cluster of red-rock formations several miles to the south.

One and a half miles south of the famous Red Rocks Amphitheater—built by the city of Denver as a public-works project

Fig. 2.5. A nineteenth-century illustration of the 200-million-year-old sandstone making up the Garden of the Gods in Colorado Springs, Colorado. (Reprinted from Hayden, Bulletin of the United States Geological and Geographical Survey of the Territories, author's collection)

in the 1930s—are a series of exposed 200-million-year-old sandstone ridges. These red rocks skirt the entire Front Range from Boulder to Colorado Springs, occasionally cropping up. In the Boulder region they're known as the Flatirons, in Denver Red Rocks, and in the Colorado Springs region they go by the name Garden of the Gods (see Figures 2.5 and 2.6). These red rocks were formed over 200 million years ago when the primeval Rocky Mountains slowly eroded away, leaving a sanded beachfront. Iron oxide in the runoff collected in the solidifying sand, giving it a reddish color. Over millions of years, more and more sediment collected over this sand, compacting it and turning it into stone. When the continent buckled and formed the present Rocky Mountains, part of this underlying strata broke through the surface and began eroding into the strange and unusual shapes we see in these locations today.

South of the Red Rocks Amphitheater on a private ranch are a cluster of protruding red stones that were once sacred to the many Indian tribes that passed through the area. Hundreds of artifacts, some dating back over five thousand years, were found at these rocks a few years ago. This was sacred space. According to longtime residents in the vicinity, this area was neutral terrain, where competing tribes could come to worship their spirits. The same was true of the Garden of the Gods area before it was turned into a nineteenth- (and twentieth-) century tourist trap.

Unfortunately, this cluster of red ridges is on private property, so access is limited,

Fig. 2.6. Cathedral Rock, Garden of the Gods, Colorado Springs. (Reprinted from Hayden, Bulletin)

if available at all. But all one need do is drive by the area some October night when the sky is clear and the moon is full. Then it will be easy to understand the mystery these stones held for generations of indigenous peoples.

The cave near Hayden Green Mountain Park was cut out of the same kind of red rocks that are found north and south of it. The cave opens up to the west. Perhaps it is aligned toward a rising moon at certain times of the year. The cave would seem admirably suited to watching the night sky over a horizon ridge. One is struck by the positioning of the cave. Why is it where it is? Why not a few feet north or south of the ridge? Perhaps this cave was a shelter for ancient travelers along the Front Range. Walk up to it and stand inside. You won't be disappointed.

Contact Persons and Organizations

Colorado Historical Society
Office of Archeological and Historic Preservation
1300 Broadway
Denver, CO 80203 -2137
(303) 866-3395

Colorado Geological Survey
1313 Sherman Street, Room 715
Denver, CO 80203
(303) 866-2611

HOGBACK STONE RUINS
Jefferson County Open Space, south of Morrison, Colorado

Site Synopsis

On top of a high mountain ridge, a series of cut stone blocks make up several enclosed rooms and walls. The stones were pried out of a nearby ledge. No tool marks on the stone are evident. The position of these ruins allows for an unobstructed spectacular view east and west of the ridge. No one knows who built this structure, or when or why.

Location

The site is located about nineteen miles southwest of Denver. From downtown Denver, take 6th Avenue west; exit onto Interstate 70 west. Stay on I-70, shortly exiting onto Route 470 south (to Colorado Springs). Stay on Route 470 for about 6.5 miles. On

your right (west), there are several eroded river cuts in the hog-backs. Turn off at the Fairplay (Route 285) exit. Continue on the ramp for approximately one mile. Pull your vehicle well off onto the grass to the right of the road shoulder just before entering the ridge rock-cut.

Walk up the ridge crossing over to the north side of the fence. This is Jefferson County Open Space land, which means there is public access. Walk along the ridge by following the fence to the spine of the hogback, taking care not to walk too closely to the edge of the cliff—it's quite a drop down to the road! About halfway up the ridge is the old Morrison Stage Coach road. Con-tinue up the ridge until the crest is reached, and follow the ridge top for half a mile. Stop by the U-shaped arrangement of stone. On a clear morning, much can be seen from this vantage point.

Considerations

There are many things to consider prior to visiting this intrigu-ing site. First and foremost is safety. You *must* contact the Jefferson County State Patrol in Lakewood, Colorado, (303) 239 - 4500, in advance, to let them know what you are doing. The dispatcher at the patrol suggests that when you park, leave a note on the dash-board stating where you are and the approximate amount of time you will be gone. In essence you are stating that your car is not abandoned (it therefore won't be towed).

Wear sturdy hiking boots. Cactus needles are everywhere in this area.

History/Background

It is difficult to believe that not much is known about this site. Although scores of hikers and hunters have passed through the ridge—beer bottles and campfire charcoal abound—there is no one source that uncovers the true meaning of this feature. (See Figures 2.7 and 2.8.)

Historians who delve into Denver's early years find tantalizing reference to hilltop ruins that were used by Indians to watch for ei-ther game or intruders. Could this site be one of them? Certainly

Fig. 2.7. A view of Hogback Ruins, facing north.

Fig. 2.8. A view of Hogback Ruins to the southwest.

Fig. 2.9. The mysterious U-shaped arrangement of stones. This view is toward the southeast.

its location affords a great view of the entire horizon. Furthermore, the nature of the construction—dry stone, no mortar—and the absence of tool marks suggests great antiquity, or at least dates the site to a time before contact with metal tools was made. (See Figure 2.9.)

A little south of the stone walls is a formation of rocks that have been carefully positioned into a U shape. They look out toward the southeastern horizon.

A thorough investigation of all ridge tops along the Front Range may turn up more of these enigmatic stone constructions (see Figure 2.10).

Fig. 2.10. Southwestern ridge-top stone structure similar to the Hogback Ruins.
(Reprinted from Hayden, *Tenth Annual Report*)

Contact Persons and Organizations

Jefferson County State Patrol
700 Kipling Avenue
Lakewood, CO 80215
 (303) 239-4500

Colorado History Museum
1300 Broadway
Denver, CO 80203-2137
 (303) 866 - 3682

Colorado Trail Foundation
548 Pine Song Trail
Golden, CO 80401

INSCRIBED CAVE (DUTCH CREEK SHELTER)
Jefferson County, Ken-Caryl Ranch, Colorado

Site Synopsis

Along one of the few remaining natural passes through the hogback formation west of Denver is a rock shelter. On the interior walls within this natural overhang of rock are dozens of near-vertical and horizontal grooves. More than a decade ago, several researchers suggested that the markings are an ancient Celtic writing system called *Ogam* (see page 26). Professional archeologists dismissed the idea, stating that the grooves were the result of local Indians sharpening their stone tools. The original researchers provided excellent evidence rebutting the tool-sharpening idea. But the controversy continues, and the cave remains filled with enigmatic slashes and grooves.

Location

The cave is located about twenty-one miles southwest of Denver. From downtown Denver, take 6th Avenue west; exit onto Interstate 70 west. Stay on I-70, shortly exiting onto Route 470 south (to Colorado Springs). Stay on Route 470 for about 8.5 miles. On your right (west), there are several eroded river cuts in the hogbacks. A highway turnoff is directly after a white bridge that traverses Dutch Creek. Hine Lake to the east is directly opposite the site (and turnoff). If you reach the Ken-Caryl Ranch exit, you've gone too far—the turnoff is about 1.5 miles north of the Ken-Caryl Ranch exit. Pull well off the road shoulder onto the grass.

Considerations

As with the hogback ruins, there are many things to consider prior to going to this intriguing site. First and foremost is safety. You *must* contact the Jefferson County State Patrol in Lakewood, Colorado, (303) 239-4500, in advance, to let them know what you are doing. The dispatcher at the patrol suggests that when you

park, leave a note on the dashboard stating where you are and the approximate amount of time you will be gone. In essence you are stating that your car is not abandoned (it therefore won't be towed). You must also get permission from the Ken-Caryl Ranch Master Association. Be prepared to give reasons why you want to visit the site and an estimate of how long your vehicle will be parked.

The only alternative to pulling off Route 470 is to park along West Bowles Avenue south of the Bergen Reservoir and hike along the eastern flank of the hogbacks. Wear high boots if you choose this option.

History/Background

As one travels south on Route 470 from Denver, the long ridge of the Dakota Hogbacks loom in the west. The hogbacks were deposited when this part of Colorado was a low-lying coastal plain with beaches and tidal flats. When the mountains west of here uplifted, the geological movement bent most of the deposits along the way.

There were several natural passes through the hogbacks before the advent of modern highways. Fast-flowing creeks cut through the sandstone, making clear avenues for foot traffic. Most of these natural passes have been widened to accommodate automobile traffic. There is one pass, however, that remains intact. Dutch Creek flows through one section of this formation. Along the northern entrance of the pass is the rock overhang. A foot trail snakes past the cave, hugging the creek.

In 1980, researchers Bill McGlone and Phil Leonard were the first to notice peculiar markings along the cave's inner wall. The markings were thought to be a form of Ogam writing. The archeological division of the Colorado Historical Society was notified, and an excavation was mounted to expose more of the cave wall's markings. Three feet of windblown cave debris was removed from the floor. This exposed much more of the slashes and grooves. No datable artifacts were uncovered. Leonard and a colleague made a tentative translation of the reputed Ogam: *May be used for shelter. This is a sheltering place for travelers in general. Whatsoever. Route-*

Fig. 2.11. Detail of markings underneath rock overhang. Note the consistency of the patterns. Some researchers claim these are the letters of an ancient Celtic alphabet, while others claim they are Indian tally markings or marks made from sharpening stone tools.

Fig. 2.12. Student researcher Anna Cayton-Holland examines details of the cave markings. Note the deep grooved incisions.

Fig. 2.13. Close-up view of the markings inside the rock overhang.

sign. To the west is the frontier-town with standing stones as boundary markers.[2]

McGlone and Leonard then mounted a Front Range search for the "city" or any other cave sites with slashes and grooves etched on any rock surface. The only other place of marked stone they found was in a cave on private property northeast of Lyons (near the Standing Stone site on the Little Thompson River).

Archeologists dismissed the Ogam interpretation of the Dutch Creek site, claiming that historical Indians sharpened their cutting tools against the rock. McGlone and Leonard then produced the most remarkable field study on the subject to date. By analyzing the grooves and depressions in scores of slash and groove sites throughout southern Colorado and elsewhere, and by comparing them with already known and recently discovered sites where tools were sharpened, they were able to conclusively state that the slashes and grooves in the Dutch Creek site and elsewhere had nothing in common with known tool-sharpening techniques. The angle of the grooves, the width, depth, and overall pattern of the Dutch Creek slashes suggest something more provocative: a conscious effort to record something. (See Figures 2.11, 2.12, and 2.13.)

Today the cave shelter continues to evoke mystery. There are hundreds of other sites throughout the American West that are similar to the Dutch Creek overhang. In southeastern Colorado alone, there are scores of such markings. Either McGlone and Leonard are correct in their interpretation or they are not. Can ancient Celtic Ogam actually be found in Colorado caves? The question almost sounds foolish. And yet, when Leonard "translated" the markings he did not know of any standing stones in the region. Our teams found such a stone not too far from a marked cave near Lyons, Colorado. Did we find one of the "frontier town" boundary markers?

Contact Persons and Organizations

Ken-Caryl Ranch Master Association
7676 Continental Divide Road
Littleton, CO 80127
(303) 979-1876

Jefferson County State Patrol
700 Kipling Avenue
Lakewood, CO 80215
(303) 239-4500

Colorado Historical Society
Office of Archeological and Historic Preservation
1300 Broadway
Denver, CO 80203-2137
(303) 866-3395
(Site Number 5JF.260)

"STANDING STONE"
Little Thompson River, northeast of Lyons, Colorado

Site Synopsis

At the bottom of a deep ravine carved out by the Little Thompson River is a ten-foot-long carved stone that once stood upright near a cool recessed pool of water. Notches are chinked in the surrounding base rock.

Location

From Denver, take Route 36 north toward Boulder. Travel through Boulder on 36 until the intersection with County Road 66. Turning west here leads to Estes Park. At the intersection light, go east for one mile before turning left (north) on Road 53 (the Longmont water tower is here). In another mile the road veers to the east (Vestal Road) and then veers north with a name change: Road 55. Travel on Road 55 for 1.5 miles. Park at the Rabbit Mountain information center. Hike from the trailhead for 2.5 miles, following the dirt trail up the ridge top. Walk along the ridge-top trail, stopping at the private-property sign. Oddly, there are no fences or blockades. The public and private road look exactly alike here; ownership rights, however, *do* change. At this point, look down the ridge top toward the winding river. Follow the barbed-wire fence down to the riverbed, making sure to stay on the public-land side of the fence. The long stone is in a recessed area near a pool of water here along the riverbed.

Considerations

It is important not to stray onto private land in your quest to visit this site. Observe and respect the posted signs.

The trip down the side of the mountain is dangerous due to the extreme slope, and the rock footing is quite loose. The climb back up the slope during a hot summer day is exhausting. Carry a water bottle.

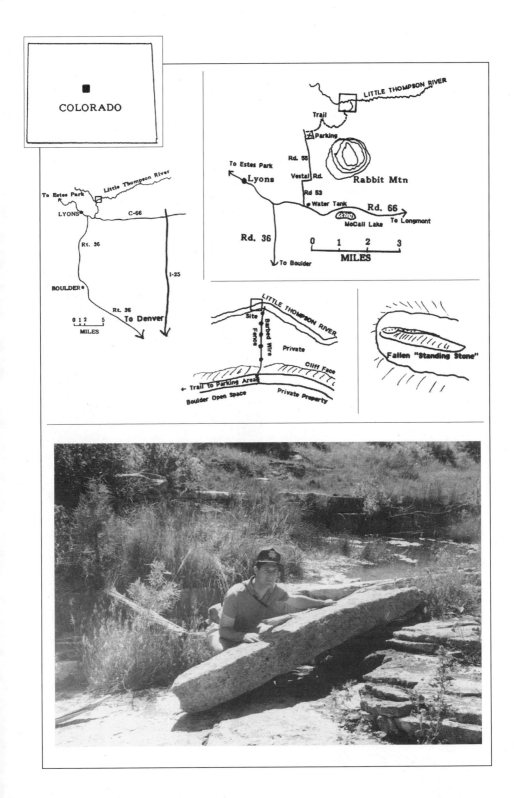

COLORADO

To Estes Park
Little Thompson River
LYONS
C-66
Rt. 36
BOULDER
Rt. 36
To Denver
I-25
0 1 2   5
MILES

LITTLE THOMPSON RIVER
Trail
Parking
Rd. 55
To Estes Park
Lyons
Vestal Rd.
Rabbit Mtn
Rd 53
Water Tank
Rd. 66
McCall Lake
To Longmont
Rd. 36
To Boulder
0   1   2   3
MILES

LITTLE THOMPSON RIVER
Site
Fence
Barbed Wire
Private
Cliff Face
← Trail to Parking Area
Boulder Open Space
Private Property

Fallen "Standing Stone"

History/Background

In 1980, researcher Phil Leonard reputedly deciphered and translated a series of markings in a cave west of Denver. His interpretation of the markings—which he claimed were a form of ancient Celtic Ogam inscriptions—made mention of a "frontier-town with standing stones as boundary markers" (see page 54).

Our teams spent several months traveling up and down the Front Range in search of anything that would fit that category. We found the stone while searching for a cave nearby that had markings similar to the Dutch Creek site near Denver.

Standing stones have a long history. They have been found throughout the world, and their uses vary among cultures. There is a solid tradition, however, of American Indian use of such stones.

Fig. 2.14. Inscribed standing stone from the Purgatoire River Valley in southeastern Colorado.

Early explorers and pioneers dutifully recorded indigenous rites at the stones (see Figure 2.14).

Contact Persons and Organizations

Boulder County Parks and Open Space
2045 13th Street
Boulder, CO 80302
(303) 441-3950
(For Open Space maps only. It is unlikely that this group knows anything about the site.)

Colorado Open Lands
1050 Walnut Street, Suite 525
Boulder, Colorado 80302
(303) 443-7347

TURTLE ROCK GEOFORMS
Red Feathers Lake, Colorado

Site Synopsis

High up in the sierra along the path of a well-known Ute trail are clusters of eroded granite blocks that seem to have defined shapes. One looks like a turtle. Depending on your viewing point and imagination, others look like dolphins, human faces, a phallus, and the like. In a nearby field are conical, moundlike structures that are probably the result of glacial outwash. Naturally carved erosion holes in many boulders have clearly placed stone blocks piled beneath them. The site is littered with prehistoric Indian artifacts, from projectile points to grinding stones. A short distance away is a gigantic perched rock. Ten miles to the east is a circle arrangement of small standing stones.

Location

From Denver, take I-25 north to Fort Collins, Road 14. From Fort Collins, travel north along Road 287 past Ted's Place to Livermore. At Livermore, turn west on C-74E. Stay on C-74E for twenty miles. Pull off the road a little west of Parvin Lake Fishery. Look back

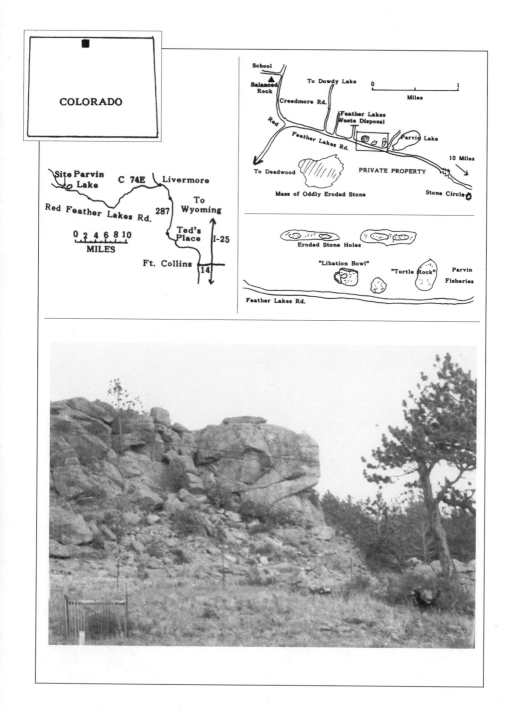

COLORADO

School
To Dowdy Lake
Balanced Rock
Creedmore Rd.
Red
Feather Lakes Waste Disposal
Feather Lakes Rd.
Parvin Lake
0 Miles 1
10 Miles
To Deadwood
PRIVATE PROPERTY
Mass of Oddly Eroded Stone
Stone Circle

Site Parvin Lake
C 74E
Livermore
To Wyoming
Red Feather Lakes Rd.
287
Ted's Place
I-25
0 2 4 6 8 10
MILES
Ft. Collins
14

Eroded Stone Holes
"Libation Bowl"
"Turtle Rock"
Parvin Fisheries
Feather Lakes Rd.

toward the fishery entrance. From this vantage, a rather large boulder jutting from an outcropping looks like a turtle. The stone holes and so-called "libation bowl" features are within the grassy areas between the fishery entrance and the Feather Lakes waste-disposal road.

From the waste disposal road, look south across C-74E. On top of the mass of oddly eroded stone is a balanced rock. This large assortment of rocks is on private property, so it is illegal to wander across the fence! Many shapes can be seen in the weathered stone, from animal forms to an enormous phalluslike stone.

Fig. 2.15. "Libation Bowl" boulder near Turtle Rock. Note the placement of the stones at the foot of the boulder.

Fig. 2.16. A close-up view, looking down, of the "Libation Bowl" boulder. Were the base stones set to prop up a ceramic pot? And if so, what liquid was being captured and why? If it was for rainwater, then it must have been for ceremonial use, for there is a stream nearby that affords a good quantity of water year-round.

Fig. 2.17. Eroded stone holes in boulders near Turtle Rock.

Considerations

Aside from the "turtle rock" and erosion-hole boulders, a good many of these objects must be viewed from the road, for they are on private property. Bring a good set of field binoculars.

History/Background

Researcher Paul Trevors of Fort Collins has spent the last ten years looking for unusual rock sites in Colorado. His labors have

Fig. 2.18. The so-called Phallus Stone. This stone seems to be a naturally eroded boulder. It is possible that some artificial carving also went into the shaping of this peculiar stone. It is big enough to sit upon, and anyone doing so with his or her back resting on the flat area will face directly toward Turtle Rock.

been successful. Trevors has plotted out dozens of seemingly ancient places that exude mystery and command respect. Turtle Rock
first came to our attention through Trevors. According to early accounts of the region, County Road 74E (Red Feathers Lake Road)
is the paved-over version of a well-used Ute hunting trail that led
from the lowlands into mountain deer and black bear country.

For most of the indigenous tribes inhabiting the American
West there was (and still is) a strong belief in the spirit world, and
that spirits inhabit everything from the smallest insects to the
largest boulder. Accordingly, great care was often taken by tribes
not to upset the cosmic balance associated with a particular place.

Fig. 2.19. Two notched boulders. One can "sight" through the two sets of notches toward
the horizon.

Offerings of corn or meat were commonly set out in open-air shrines at these places.

The rocks at Red Feathers Lake were carved into their shapes by a combination of glacial meltdown and thousands of years of frost, thaw, and wind erosion. This natural sculpting only heightened the belief among the indigenous population that the gods must inhabit this place, for the forms are remarkably realistic. Evidence of some type of human use comes from a variety of indirect evidence. The Turtle Rock site is located directly along the ancient trail. Prehistoric stone tools found lying next to the assortment of rocks clearly indicates early Indian interest here. Arrangements of stone slabs at the bases of circular depressions in boulders suggest something important—perhaps a clay pot was placed below to catch rainwater, or perhaps there was a more mystical meaning to the arrangement.

The depressions, also known as "bath tub rocks," were formed during heavy rainfalls, when water cut through the surface shell into the disintegrated rock beneath, rapidly removing the loosened rock and fashioning flat-bottomed depressions. These usually have a low outlet through which the sands have been washed.

In a private field across from the turtle form is a large cluster of rocks. On the top of the mass of stone is a perched boulder. Scattered north and south of this glacial arrangement are stones that have been naturally formed into a variety of shapes. Some look like vast gun sights; one looks like a giant phallus. The place speaks of ancient mystery.

Up the road from Turtle Rock is a large boulder balanced on several smaller rocks. While clearly the result of a massive melting glacier, the site still suggests mystery, serendipity, and possible use by the ancient peoples who passed this way.

Ten miles to the east of the Turtle Rock site, on private land near a house, is what appears to be a circular arrangement of standing stones. The stones are between two and three feet tall. They suggest placement by human hands at some time in the dim past. (See Figures 2.15, 2.16, 2.17, 2.18, and 2.19.)

Contact Persons and Organizations

Colorado Geological Survey
1313 Sherman Street, Room 715
Denver, CO 80203
(303) 866-2611

PERCHED ROCKS
Rawah Wilderness Area, Roosevelt National Forest

Site Synopsis

Several granite boulders are perched on three and four base rocks in a seemingly organized manner.

Location

Travel north from Fort Collins along Route 287, turning west onto Road 14 (at Ted's Place). Travel west for approximately forty-five miles. Turn north on County Road 103, driving for fifteen miles along the Laramie River. Turn west onto County Road 190 and drive for three miles, passing over Stub Creek and Jinks Creek. Pull off the road at Jinks Creek (there's a public campground there). Put on your pack and travel south along Pack Trail #963 (Link Trail). Nine miles into the hike will bring you to the Rawah Lakes (follow the Rawah Creek southwest—the trail moves off to the east). A series of perched boulders can be seen a few hundred yards to the northwest of the lake.

Considerations

Because this is a national forest, take out what you take in—leave no trash or debris. Also be on guard against mountain cats.

Give yourself plenty of time to hike these trails: Take a pack and sleeping gear for at least two days and one night. The scenery is breathtaking.

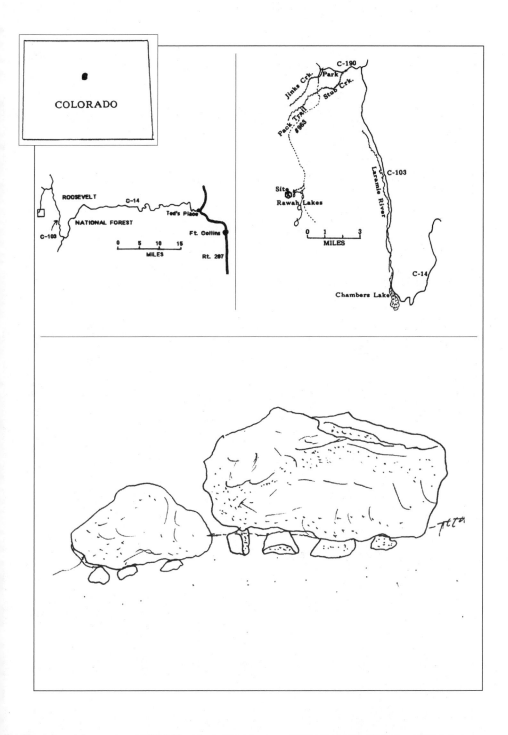

History/Background

Perched rocks are scattered throughout most of the national forests in the Rocky Mountain West. In fact, any place where glacial meltdown occurred, perched rocks are found. They are geological evidence of activity more than ten thousand years ago.

Many indigenous tribes placed great spiritual value on these stones, because they were thought to be gifts from the spirit world. According to early explorers, many of these perched-rock sites were used as markers in vision quests—ritual roamings by young men in search of their individual guiding spirits.

Contact Persons and Organizations

United States Government
Department of the Interior, National Park Service
12795 West Alameda
Lakewood, CO 80215
(303) 969-2000

United States Government
Department of Agriculture, Forest Service
Rocky Mountain Regional Office
11177 West 8th Avenue
Denver, CO
(303) 236-9435

Colorado Geological Survey
1313 Sherman Street, Room 715
Denver, CO 80203
(303) 866-2611

STONE CYLINDERS
East Brush Creek, Eagle County, Colorado

Site Synopsis

A calcareous siltstone bed sixteen feet thick contains many cylindrical or columnlike structures. The cylindrical structures are all perpendicular to the bedding, which makes it highly unusual. Their composition is identical to that of the rest of the bed: coarse-grained quartzites, conglomerates, and limestone. Diameters range from less than one inch to two feet. The cylinders cross the bedding indiscriminately, and all seem to extend to the base of the bed. They are erratically distributed but are confined within several hundred feet along the outcrop.

Location

From Denver, travel west on I-70 toward the ski resort of Vail. Continue past Vail for another forty miles, exiting at Eagle. Pass over the Eagle River and through the town's Main Street, watching for signs to Sylvan Lake–Brush Creek Road (C-307). Take C-307 south for ten miles. The road will split into West and East Brush Creek roads. Take the unpaved East Brush Creek Road (Road 415), the road on the left. In 1.1 miles, park on a small dirt extension of the road to the south (toward the creek). A gully should appear across the road. A broad expanse of tan rock face is directly east of the gully.

Walk into the gully, scanning both sides for evidence of long cylindrical formations in the maroon rock. Occasionally, a weathered rock slab can be found on the gully bottom. Continue walking, watching for falling rocks. The climb gets rather steep as you continue. Be prepared to scale some rocks. The longest cylinders are farther up the mountain within this narrow gorge.

Considerations

As with all geological sites, sample-taking is not permitted! Observe this curiosity but leave it in place. Watch for falling slabs of rock!

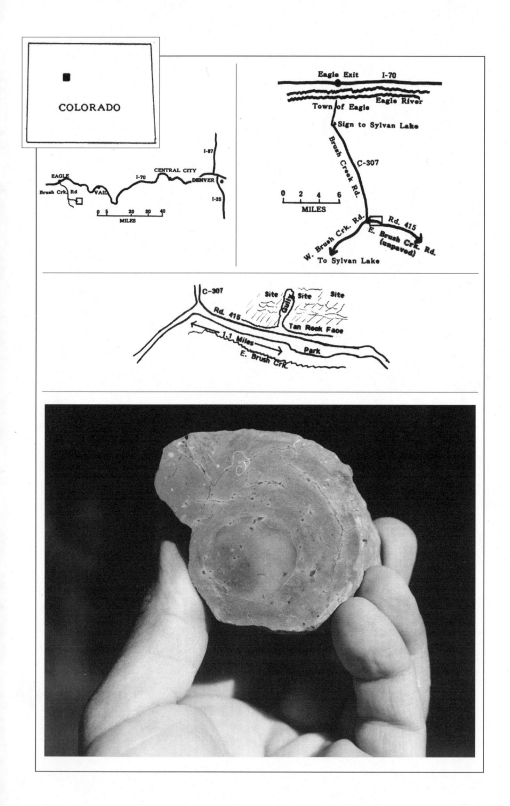

Fig. 2.20. Drawing of a
cylinder within a siltstone bed.

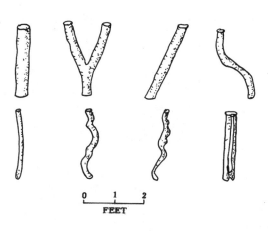

Fig. 2.21. Forms of stone cylinders
(after Gabelman).

Fig. 2.22. A curved stone cylinder from the site gulch.

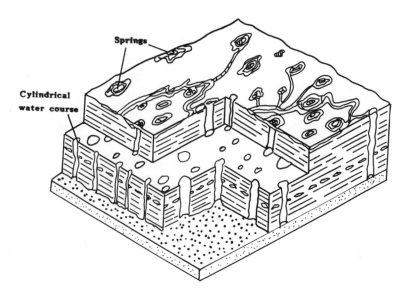

Fig. 2.23. *Hypothetical conception of cylinder formation from spring channels (after Gabelman).*

History/Background

Geologists have observed cylinderlike structures in rock bedding planes for years. The geological literature is filled with examples from around the country. Columns similar to the Colorado examples have been found in upper New York State, Ontario, Canada, and elsewhere. As with most anomalies, there are several explanations for the origin. Do note, however, that professional geologists differ—sometimes vehemently—in their interpretations.

The Colorado columns are thought to be 200-million-year-old fossil springs or quicksand pipes in which surface mud compacted (see Figures 2.20, 2.21, and 2.22). Somehow the natural bedding within the pipes was destroyed by water quickly rising up through the mud (see Figure 2.23).This said, it is unclear why the columns retained their integrity.

Diameters of the exposed cylinders range from one-half to eight inches. Their length varies from a few inches up to four feet. Good examples can be found along the gully bottom along the outcrop. The rock-bed color fluctuates from maroon to shades of cream. Occasionally the cylinders are lighter in color; this is the result of iron oxide leaching from the cylinders.

Contact Persons and Organizations

Good descriptions of these types of structures can be found in the following source: John W. Gabelman. "Cylindrical Structures in Permian (?) Siltstone, Eagle County, Colorado." *Journal of Geology*, 63, no. 3 (1955): 214–227.

Colorado Geological Survey
1313 Sherman Street, Room 715
Denver, CO 80203
(303) 866-2611

FULFORD CAVE
Eagle County, Colorado

Site Synopsis

At an elevation of 9,880 feet, Fulford Cave is the eighth largest cave in Colorado. In 1959, over 2,600 feet of it had been mapped. There still are vast sections of the cave waiting to be explored. Gaping crevices, vast spaces, stalactites, and narrow passages make up the mystery of this cave. Its gorges range greatly in size: some are three hundred feet long, and others are over sixty feet high. One three-hundred-foot section of the cave has a roaring stream that emerges at a surface spring in the neighboring campground.

Location

From Denver, travel west on I-70 toward the ski resort at Vail. Continue past Vail for another forty miles, exiting at Eagle. Pass over the Eagle River and through the town's Main Street; watch

COLORADO

I-87

CENTRAL CITY

EAGLE

I-70

DENVER

Brush Crk. Rd

VAIL

I-25

0 5   20   30   40
MILES

Eagle Exit   I-70

Eagle River

Town of Eagle

Sign to Sylvan Lake

Brush Creek Rd.

C-307

0   2   4   6
MILES

Rd. 415

W. Brush Crk. Rd.

E. Brush Crk. Rd.
(unpaved)

To Sylvan Lake

To Fulford

8.2 miles to
Brush Crk.
Rd.

Rd. 415

Sign: Fulford Cave

.7 mile Trail to Cave

Lower Opening

Upper Opening

Park

Beaver Pond

1 Mile

Benches

for signs to Sylvan Lake–Brush Creek Road (C-307). Take C-307 south for ten miles. The road will split into West and East Brush Creek roads. Take the unpaved East Brush Creek Road (Road 415)—the road on the left.

After the winter-spring frost-and-thaw cycle, the road can get rutted with bumps—drive slowly. Continue for 6.2 miles along East Brush Creek Road (Road 415). At that distance the road will split: the north route goes to Fulford; the eastern route continues on to Fulford Cave. Drive a mile along this road and park along the Beaver Pond. The trailhead to the cave is marked.

The trail to Fulford Cave is a little less than a mile, but it zigzags up a steep incline. Be prepared to stop and rest. The view near the top is superb. The timbered entranceway along the trail should not be entered; it was apparently dug in the late 1890s by a miner. Continue past this, looking for the mountain face as a guide marker. At the top of the trail two openings can be seen: they are the lower and upper entranceways. Climb down the laddered entranceway. Be sure you have proper spelunking equipment. Fulford Cave is not for the casual day hiker!

Considerations

Caving is a dangerous activity. The dependency on artificial light makes for some special considerations: Always carry *several* powerful flashlights, with extra batteries and bulbs wrapped in a waterproof pouch. Some caving professionals recommend carbide lamps as a primary light source, with candles and flashlights as a backup. The cold temperatures of a cave may cause hypothermia. Also, the mud and humidity create very slippery conditions. It is therefore recommended that warm, durable, fast-drying clothes and a hat be worn. A hard helmet will help prevent head wounds. Ankle-high waterproof boots are also recommended. A first aid kit and drinking water is required equipment. Ropes, tear-resistant guide string, as well as a compass, gloves, knee pads, and a watch are also necessary.

Never go caving alone! It is also a good idea to let others know where you are going and when you plan to return. And finally, if you are not thoroughly prepared to go caving—if you do not have the above required equipment—*do not go into a cave*. Serious injury or death can result. It's happened too often.

It is a crime to take any specimen from a cave in the United States. Furthermore, Colorado has a revised statute that makes it a misdemeanor to do so. The penalty includes a five-hundred-dollar fine and a ninety-day jail sentence. Leave all cave features intact. Take pictures but nothing else!

History/Background

Fulford Cave was named after the historic town of Fulford, located a few miles away. In 1890, a Captain Nolan Smith claimed to be the original discover of the site. By 1892, however, a fellow by the name of Maxwell filed a mining claim on the area surrounding the cave. He said that he found rich silver ore deposits and veins within the cave (in actuality, there are none). The pit entrance and timbered entrance chamber were apparently dug by Maxwell.

A February 5, 1893, edition of the *Rocky Mountain News* lists the earliest description of the cave:

A HOLLOW MOUNTAIN

Discovery of a Wonderful Cave
Near Brush Creek in Eagle County

Stalactite and Stalagmite Formations
That Dazzle the Eye and Bewilder
One with Beauty

Underground Streams and Lakes—Lacework
in the Rocks—Thrones of Crystal
Whiteness—A Marvel

During the year 1941, pioneer spelunker Seward S. Cramer of Chicago, Illinois, visited the cave for the Explorers Club of America. Cramer was on a national tour to visit all of the 610 caves then known in the United States. In the late 1950s, John Thrailkill of the Colorado Grotto National Speleological Society did the preliminary mapping of Fulford Cave. Since that time more pathways have been charted.

Caves are amazing places to explore. Being inside the bowels of the earth for any length of time makes one fully appreciate the wonders of our light-saturated above-ground world. It is not surprising that many cultures worldwide consider dark caverns to be the habitation sites of evil spirits and demons. A cave is an alien environment, unlike anything on the surface.

There are many cave formations to be seen at this site, as well as at most caves. Centuries of percolation from the surrounding limestone have coated the interior of Fulford Cave with a

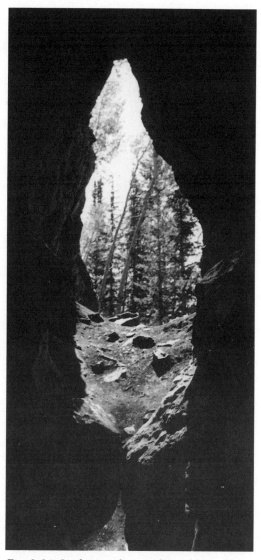

Fig. 2.24. Looking to the outside world from the entrance of Fulford Cave.

whitewash. There are abundant amounts of stalactites (dripstones that hang from the ceiling) and stalagmites (dripstones that build up from the ground). Various types of minerals found in the bedrock, such as iron and galena, have colored several of the cave walls.

Assorted indigenous Indian tribes in Colorado and elsewhere in the West used caves as places for spiritual renewal. These sites were sacred places that native priests and shamans would go to to commune with the spirits, seek guidance, and make offerings. Although there is no direct evidence that Fulford Cave was used by any Colorado tribes, considering its vast size and the enormous length of time Indians have been in the region, it is likely that some people in the dim past saw the cave opening, entered, and saw otherworldly wonders. (See Figure 2.24.)

Contact Persons and Organizations

An excellent description of this cave and others in Colorado can be found in the now out-of-print *Caves of Colorado*, by Lloyd E. Parris (Boulder, Colo.: Pruett Publishing Company, 1973).

Colorado Geological Survey
1313 Sherman Street, Room 715
Denver, Colorado 80203
(303) 866- 2611

United States Department of Interior, Geological Survey
Denver Federal Center, Box 25286
Denver, CO 80225
(303) 236-7477

PAWNEE BUTTES
Pawnee National Grasslands, north of New Raymer, Colorado

Site Synopsis

In northeastern Colorado about one hundred miles east of the Rocky Mountains sit three eroded flat-topped hills (*buttes*) that rise abruptly from the surrounding prairie. Dating to the Oligocene Epoch (a geological time period dating to 35 million years ago), these sandstone mounds are the product of hundreds of thousands of years of wind and water erosion. Falcons, eagles, and other birds of prey rest atop the weather-scarred buttes. These prominent stone structures—they can be seen for miles—are the resistant remains of a wide-ranging plateau. Tucked into the decomposing structures and scarred gullies are the fossil remains of giant creatures that once roamed the earth.

Location

The Pawnee Buttes are about a two- to three-hour drive from downtown Denver. Follow Interstate 25 north to I-76, and take the Fort Morgan exit (east). Continue onward, exiting at Fort Morgan, taking Colorado 52 (C-52) north for twenty-six miles. Be aware that this road is closed periodically due to heavy snowdrifts or high winds. At the end of C-52, turn left (west) onto Colorado 14 (C-14). Travel for two miles toward New Raymer, watching for Weld County Road 129. The road is marked by a street sign (it's easy to miss). From this point on, the road is not paved. In fact, it gets progressively less gravel-based and more dirt-based as one drives along. Travel for 6.5 miles on Road 129 before turning left (west) onto Road 110, following the sign to Pawnee Buttes. After one mile the road veers off to the right; again, follow the sign here for Pawnee Buttes. Travel the next two miles very slowly over the dirt road before parking on a trailhead near a windmill (don't make the first stop—a scenic lookout for the trailhead—drive another hundred yards or so to the parking area, which is on the west side of the buttes).

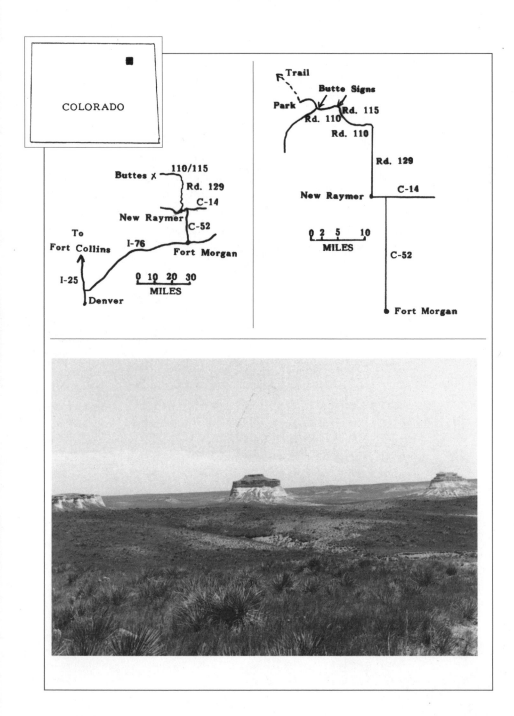

COLORADO

Trail

Park

Butte Signs

Rd. 115

Rd. 110

Rd. 110

Rd. 129

New Raymer

C-14

0 2 5 10
MILES

C-52

Fort Morgan

Buttes X

110/115

Rd. 129

C-14

New Raymer

C-52

To
Fort Collins

I-76

Fort Morgan

I-25

Denver

0 10 20 30
MILES

Considerations

The last part of the trip can cause problems if it has recently rained. Dirt and gravel make for deep mud ruts. In fact, even four-wheel-drive vehicles can slip and slide off the dirt path. Check with the National Weather Service (see information later in this chapter) before leaving home. Be careful to drive very slowly along Road 110 near the end of the trip. The road is narrow and there are several blind spots as one approaches turns and road mounds.

Although it is fun to search along the numerous gullies (eroded pathways formed by flash floods and river-scarring), rattlesnakes like to slither in the hot sandy bottoms.

Water is a concern, because there are no facilities at the site. Bring lots of potable water and food with you if you wish to hike around the buttes or stay overnight.

Overnight camping is permitted as long as one stays more than one hundred feet from the base of the buttes. Bring along a stove, tent, and binoculars. The canopy of stars is spectacular here, because there is no light pollution. In fact, for those with a cursory knowledge of key stars, seeing so many stars in the heavens can create problems—it's even difficult to locate the Big Dipper, that perennial of the urban sky!

Artifact collecting—be it fossil, bone, or prehistoric Indian—is prohibited on federal lands. Look lovingly upon these remnants of an ancient, alien past, but leave all items in the ground!

History/Background

The Pawnee Buttes were the object of sacred worship among the Cheyenne and Arapaho Plains Indians, who camped near the buttes from around 1820 through the 1870s (see Figures 2.25 and 2.26). The stark isolation and difficulty of getting to the site—even today—make for a mystical place. At nighttime under a full moon it is easy to understand why. The butte site evokes a strange feeling of wildness that is literally millions of years old.

Contrary to the name, the Pawnee Indians had little to do with the Buttes. Recent excavations by archeologists from the

Fig. 2.25. A nineteenth-century illustration of a table butte with geology very similar to the Pawnee Buttes. (Reprinted from Hayden, Bulletin)

Fig. 2.26. An Indian camp similar to those that were at the Pawnee Buttes. (Reprinted from Vivian, Wanderings in the Western Land, author's collection)

Fig. 2.27. Eroded streambed at the base of Pawnee Buttes.

University of Northern Colorado have turned up stone tools, charcoal, broken pottery, and butchered bison bones dating back more than six thousand years. In fact, stone spear tips found at the grassland site are a type usually found in the mountains, over one hundred miles from the buttes. This suggests either great tribe movement or an extensive trade route.

The archeological finds indicate that indigenous peoples were camping at the buttes seasonally for a very long time. No doubt they were following the migration routes of herd animals.

The buttes are the product of millions of years of erosion. Within the white chalky peaks are the remains of giant extinct

browsers with names like *Brontops* and *Brontotherium*—rhinocer-
oslike creatures that pulled leaves from tall shrubs and low trees
with their lips. The fossils of strange, saber-toothed doglike creatures can also be found within the stone matrix. Known as *Hyaen-
odon*, these bulky, long-headed beasts had teeth resembling those
of present-day hyenas. Fossils of primitive three-toed horses, giraf-
felike camels, large pigs, and extinct forms of deer can also be
found in abundance.

Pawnee Buttes is a place where the spirits of millions of prehistoric creatures congregate. It is a humbling experience to be in the
place where these strange and wondrous beings lived and died.
(See Figure 2.27.)

Contact Persons and Organizations

United States Government
Department of Commerce, National Weather Service
10230 Smith Road
Denver, CO 80239
(303) 398-3964

United States Government
Department of Agriculture, Forest Service
Rocky Mountain Regional Office
11177 West 8th Avenue
Denver, CO 80215
(303) 236-9435

Colorado Geological Survey
1313 Sherman Street, Room 715
Denver, CO 80203
(303) 866-2611

United States Department of Interior, Geological Survey
Denver Federal Center, Box 25286
Denver, CO 80225
(303) 236-7477

Southeastern Colorado

Colorado is a state of extremes. The western fringe moves upward into the grandeur of the Rocky Mountains, which themselves rise over fourteen thousand feet before terminating in glacially scarred peaks. Moving east of the high mountains toward the Front Range—that area between the highest peaks and the hogbacks west of Denver—one is struck by the flatness of the  high plains. But traveling eastward, one also is struck by the strangeness of the southeastern plain: It is flat, arid, and isolated. The vastness of the buffalo grass and sage, however, is broken by the unexpected—the Purgatoire River Valley. This area demands attention, for, seemingly, out of the flat terrain rise cliffs over two hundred feet high.

Strewn along the Purgatoire canyon walls, amid rattlesnakes and desert scrub brush, are the remnants of an ancient people: There are thousands of intriguing glyphlike marks covering hundreds of feet of rock face. Unfortunately, the most impressive sites are located near dry arroyos (streambeds) on private ranches. To get to them you need permission from the owners, as well as a high-clearance four-wheel-drive vehicle. Once permission is obtained, it is not uncommon to spend an hour or two slowly crawling over a dusty, rutted ranch road getting to a site. In traveling on these roads, miles from the beaten path, with no one, not a house or person, in sight for miles, care must be taken to check frequently for rain clouds. A sudden storm can quickly flood dry arroyos, covering up the road and perhaps your vehicle as well. Furthermore, dusty roads plus water means impossibly slippery and deep mud roads.

Throughout this vast area are multiple canyons of the Purgatoire River. There are many anomalous archeological sites scattered about. A number of local researchers—Bill McGlone, in particular—have come upon a rather novel interpretation of the assortment of sunlight-caves and marked stones: Namely, that the sites may represent the work of ancient Old World explorers!

An 1845 print of a canyoned creek of the Purgatoire River. On many of these rock walls are thousands of stone carvings. On some of the canyon promontories are unexplained, isolated stone circles. (Reprinted from Abert, Communicating a report of an expedition, *author's collection)*

At the top of these cliffs above a tributary of the Purgatoire River are hundreds of petroglyphs. On the entire top side of these rocks and scattered throughout the surrounding arroyo are hundreds of strange carvings.

In many parts of southeastern Colorado where wind and water have patiently eroded away eons-old rock surfaces, one encounters such strange geology as this: a fossilized imprint of a 300-million-year-old sea worm track. This one was found in a dried-out arroyo thirty miles southeast of La Junta, Colorado.

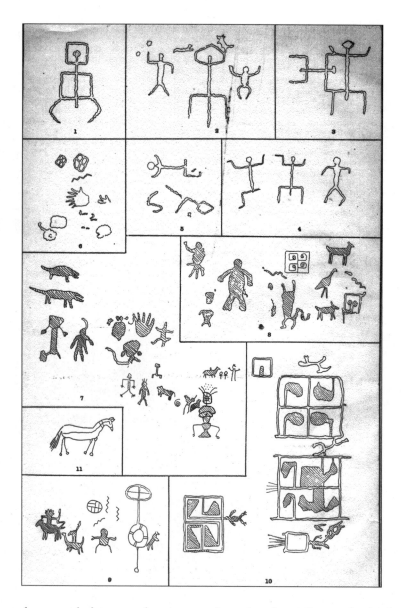

"To us, these petroglyphs are not the remnants of some long-lost civilization that has been dead for many years. They are part of our living culture," Herman Agoyo, former chairman of the All Indian Pueblo Council. (Ancient and modern petroglyphs reprinted from Hayden, Tenth Annual Report)

STONE CIRCLES
Apishapa Wildlife Area, Colorado

Site Synopsis

In southeastern Colorado, on the high plains among the sage and cactus, a circle of upright standing stones rests in mute testimony to past human activity. The circle of stones stands in a petroglyph-strewn canyon carved out by the Apishapa River. The builders and purpose of these mysterious prehistoric remains are unknown.

Location

From Denver, go south on Colorado Boulevard to I-25. Take I-25 south past Pueblo to Highway 50 East (the La Junta exit) to Fowler. Head south on Highway 167 (approximately one mile west of Fowler) to Highway 10. Go southwest on Highway 10 toward Walsenburg for eight miles. At this point, there is a gravel road running south (Whiterock Road). Turn onto this road and travel for fourteen miles until Road 94.0 is reached. Turn west onto this road. Travel until Road 94.0 crosses the river three times. At the third crossing, park and hike northwest along the river for three miles to the Apishapa Canyon. Below the stone circle cliff (also referred to as the "Snake Blakesly Site") is a large meadow.

Considerations

This trip is best set up for overnight camping. Take appropriate tents and sleeping bags. Flashlights, food, water, and first aid kits are recommended. Sturdy walking boots—not sneakers—are recommended due to the cactus.

Be sure to check with local ranchers before setting off the road. A good section of this region is privately owned. The relevant Colorado topographic maps are: Western U.S. 1:250,000; Trinidad 13-8' County Map *or* Sun Valley Ranch County Quad 7.5' series.

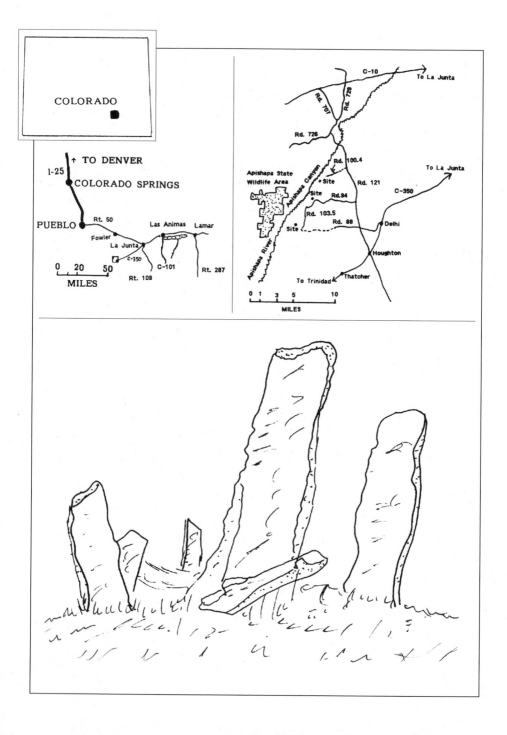

Fig. 2.28. An eighteenth-century French illustration of Virginia Indians dancing around standing totem poles. (Reprinted from Lubbock, The Origins of Civilization and the Primitive Condition of Man, author's collection)

As with all ancient sites, care must be taken not to disturb anything. Experience the wonders of this strange and peaceful place, but take your trash out with you!

History/Background

Stone circles have a long unexplained history in this country. For a good many modern archeologists they are a largely unrecognized source of information. This, no doubt, was because in the past (and today, too) too many scientists, amazingly, dismissed them as random products of glacial meltdown!

There are scores of stone circles along the Purgatoire River Valley. Although attempts have been made to map out these sites, most have not been recorded due to their location on private property. This, unfortunately, has deterred serious investigation of these enigmatic structures.

If we look elsewhere in the country and world, we see that many cultures, some up to relatively recent times, used arrangements of

Fig. 2.29. Engraving of an ancient stone circle in southern India. (Reprinted from Lubbock, *The Origins of Civilization*)

circles for religious dances. A wonderful woodcut from an eighteenth-century French description of Virginia details natives dancing around standing wood posts with carved faces on top (see Figure 2.28). In ancient India, along high flattened peaks, people worshipped by dancing in the midst of small stone circles (see Figure 2.29).

The Colorado stone circles are always situated on rather barren high promontories in clear view of the horizon. They appear in clusters on both sides of the river valley. Some of the stones are rather large while others are no more than a foot above the ground. It is difficult to say what they were used for. A scientist from the University of Colorado at Denver plotted out one of the sites a few years back and could find no obvious alignments with astronomical features. We are still left with the fact that these mysterious circles of stone are usually located atop the highest point available. Clearly, the people who constructed them had *something* in mind. Perhaps the view.

It may be enlightening to consider the modern Pueblo traditions of the central New Mexico area, where stone shrines were placed on top of high peaks in clear view of the four cardinal directions. These were very powerful and sacred sites. But as yet, no one has any absolute idea what the southeastern Colorado stone circles represent. They remain as enigmatic today as when the first white pioneers discovered them in the early 1800s.

Even so, sporadic excavations by various archeological groups have revealed some information about these sites. Survey work during the late 1980s and early 1990s by the archeological branch of the Colorado Historical Society in Denver suggests that some of these stone circle sites were foundations for huts. Post holes were found next to a few of the ringed stones. The implication is that poles were inserted into the holes, bent over toward a central standing stone, and some type of covering, perhaps grass, was placed on top. In a few of these sites, mortars and pestles, along with flint flakes and carving knives, were found. So it seems that a few of these sites were used as camping stations. The human groups clearly didn't live at the sites year-round—there wasn't enough archeological debris to suggest it. Furthermore, the stone

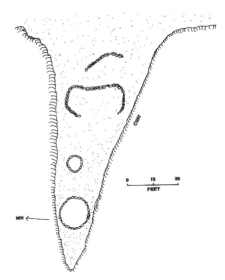

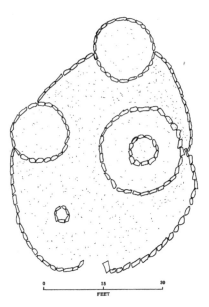

Fig. 2.30. The Apishapa River Valley stone circle site. (After Renaud, The Archaeological Survey of Colorado, Second Report)

Fig. 2.31. Stone enclosures, Apishapa Valley. (After Renaud, Archaeological Survey, Second Report)

circle sites seem vaguely similar to those found in the Oklahoma panhandle area. A migration of people from the panhandle area into the Purgatoire River Valley sometime around A.D. 700 is the going theory among archeologists to explain these weird sites. Perhaps.

There are still stone sites that have no central column, sites with triangularly carved stones carefully laid in rings, and multitudes of circle sites high above rock wall overhangs lining the Purgatoire River Valley. While we have functional gleanings from some of these sites, it would be inaccurate to classify all as camping spots. Something more provocative was going on at these ruins.

Closer to the Front Range are a series of stone enclosures and circles that were first examined in the 1930s by Dr. E. B. Renaud, professor of anthropology at the University of Denver. In a bold move for the times, Dr. Renaud logged over ten thousand miles in the early 1930s surveying and recording archeological sites throughout eastern Colorado. He recognized early on that most of the interest in the state centered around the impressive ruins of the southwest—the Mesa Verde complex. During his surveys, Dr. Renaud detailed many sites along the Apishapa (see Figures 2.30 and 2.31). He also recorded several stone circle sites north and east of Canon City (see Figure 2.32). North of Webster Park, on cliffs above Wilson Creek, are several rectangular enclosures of stone. Renaud wrote of them:

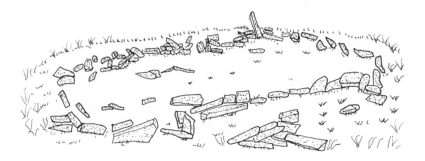

Fig. 2.32. A sketch of the stone circle east of Canon City, Colorado.

They are partly made of rocks in their natural positions and of blocks of sandstone piled up on the other sides to complete the enclosures. They average ...[six feet] by...[four feet]...Large pine trees are scattered on the top of the bluff and among the enclosures as if they had grown since the fences were put up, which would also suggest antiquity. At one place there is a low and broad fence made of small quartzite rocks. It extends for a length of about 15 paces. At one end there is a circle with a tree growing in the middle of it.[3]

Northeast of Canon City along Turkey Creek, an area now part of the Fort Carson Military Reservation, Renaud mentions several rather large stone enclosures:

From this site one enjoys an excellent view south and S.E. across the Arkansas valley, which is quite broad there, and towards the mountains...this place is a very good lookout...It is also a stronghold, impregnable on two sides as a result of almost inaccessible slopes and fortified on the other sides by broad and high stone fences.[4]

In 1987 and 1990, Centennial Archaeology, Inc., a research group based in Fort Collins, Colorado, submitted detailed surveys and test excavation reports to the United States Army, among others, regarding their work in the Turkey Canyon area. These reports are *must* reading for anyone interested in these bizarre stone enclosures.

Contact Persons and Organizations

Colorado Geological Survey
1313 Sherman Street, Room 715
Denver, CO 80203
(303) 866-2611

Christian J. Zier, et. al. "Historic Preservation Plan for Fort Carson Military Reservation, Colorado," Contract no. CX-1200-5-A006. Fort Collins, Colo.: Centennial Archaeology, Inc., 1987.

Margaret Van Ness, et. al. "Archaeological Survey and Test Excavation in the Turkey Canyon Area, Fort Carson Military Reservation, Pueblo and El Paso Counties, Colorado." Contract no. CX 1200-7-B066. Fort Collins, Colo.: Centennial Archaeology, Inc., 1990.

VOGEL CANYON PETROGLYPHS
Comanche National Grassland, south of La Junta, Colorado

Site Synopsis

In southeastern Colorado along an eroded tributary canyon of the Purgatoire River Valley are a series of high sandstone cliffs and caves. Along the flat walls of this canyon are multitudes of pecked and incised carvings made by a people who lived here thousands of years ago. Some of the petroglyphs are reminiscent of those found elsewhere in the Southwest. Others are found nowhere else. Evidence of something important happening here in the distant past is all around the valley—there are rock carvings everywhere. The assorted petroglyphs speak to all who take the time to walk through this mysteriously beautiful canyon.

Location

From Denver, take Interstate 25 south to Pueblo. At Pueblo, exit onto Route 50 east, going toward La Junta. Drive until you reach La Junta. Take Road 109 south for sixteen miles until you reach the hamlet of Higbee. There is a southward turnoff at this point, and signs point toward Vogel Canyon. Follow this road for about three miles before turning off to the well-marked parking area. Hike in one-half mile, following the cairn-marked trail. The expanse of canyon wall will be on your left.

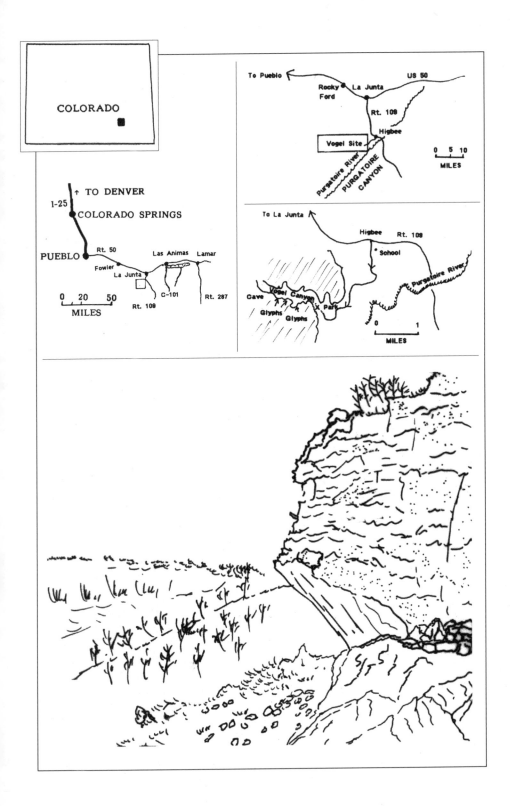

Considerations

Almost all of the canyons south of La Junta have petroglyph carvings. Some are more impressive than others. Although the Vogel Canyon site is open to the public, most rock carvings are on private ranches. Permission to go on a posted ranch trail is essential before entering someone's property. Although it is unlikely that any serious confrontation will occur, ranchers have every right to assume trespassers on their property are poaching and to take the necessary steps to get them off. It is recommended that you stick to the public access sites listed in this book. If you want to see more, it is essential that you contact the landowner before stepping onto fenced-in land.

Although it is open to the public, very few people walk into the Vogel site. You can expect to see one or two hikers along the trail.

If you visit this site during the summer months, always remember to pack as much water as possible, for you will lose a significant amount of water in the hot prairie sun. Wrap-around-the-waist water-bottle carriers are ideal for this type of hiking, for you will need your hands for climbing. Take frequent rests in the cool shade of a canyon wall, but watch out for rattlers! Always carry a long stick to tap the ground ahead of you as you walk. And carry a snake-bite kit.

History/Background

The ranches around southeastern Colorado were homesteaded after the Civil War. Due to the Indian threat and the lack of water away from the canyons and tributaries, the area was not hospitable for large grazing ranches. That changed with the advent of barbed wire and the windmill. Barbed wire allowed the enclosure of huge tracts of land to contain roaming cattle. The simple windmill and its on-off pump also led to major changes in land usage. A windmill pumps up water from the aquifer below-ground, filling a basin. When the water in the basin reaches a certain level, the pump shuts off, stopping the windmill fan from turning. When cattle

Vogel Canyon. On these walls are scores of inexplicable carvings. One rock wall has a series of markings that look like sheet music! There are two large caves in the canyon that have seen very little systematic exploration.

drink from the basin, lowering the water level, the windmill blades start moving again. This marvelous invention allowed for open-range grazing over thousands of acres of land with little concern on the part of the rancher, at least until roundup time.

The Purgatoire River was once home to thousands of white settlers, as evidenced by the high number of farm and ranch foundations found there. And before that, it was home to various American Indian groups for thousands of years, as may be seen by the staggering number of rock carvings in the region. But this area is much less well known than the Four Corners region of Colorado, where the preponderance of Anasazi ruins—at Mesa Verde and other sites—have been known since the late 1840s. Not much archeological excavation work has gone on in southeastern Colorado. This will change, for although the ruins are not as numerous here, the obsession of the ancient people to cover their canyon walls with thousands of marks speaks in a way ruins do not. The placement of the carvings, the repetition of certain design motifs, their very style, suggests some type of message is contained within. All we need is the code. One man in particular is hot on the trail.

Bill McGlone is a retired engineer who moved to southeastern Colorado over ten years ago to study the Purgatoire Valley petroglyphs. McGlone is convinced that some of the markings—the ones that are unique to Colorado—are a form of alphabet of an ancient writing system. McGlone has cautiously and meticulously put together reams of comparative data. Specifically, McGlone claims to have found canyon-wall markings that seem to be Ogam (vertical slashes across a horizontal groove) and symbols that were used in ancient Libya!

Although symbols in one culture could easily be independently invented and used simultaneously in a far-removed isolated culture, McGlone has carefully detailed the repetition frequency of these symbols and has compared them with examples of writing from other parts of the world. Amazingly, the similarity appears to be more than a chance occurrence. His work, in collaboration with a variety of specialists, is detailed in his latest book, *Ancient American Inscriptions*. It makes for some provocative reading.

Not surprisingly, most western archeologists dismiss all of this as so much folderol. They see the petroglyphs in the broader context of indigenous Native American culture. The symbols that are unlike other petroglyphs in the West are considered to be merely unrecognized markings—with enough study, these petroglyphs will be seen to be part of the repertoire of prehistoric Indian culture.

At first glance it does seem a bit preposterous that Old World explorers could suddenly wind up in Colorado. As stated earlier, where are the habitation sites, the garbage, the burials? McGlone and his colleagues have no answers. They merely point to the markings and their astonishing similarity to various ancient Old World scripts.

Either way one interprets the enormous amount of marked canyon walls found in southeastern Colorado, the fact remains that their meaning is a total mystery. It's been argued that most petroglyph sites are in fact sacred sites where ancient people went to experience visions—to commune with the gods.

Contact Persons and Organizations

An excellent place to examine McGlone's work is his recently published book, *Ancient Inscriptions: Plow Marks or History?* (Sutton, Mass.: Early Sites Research Society, 1994).

Colorado Division of Wildlife
6060 Broadway
Denver, CO 80216

HICKLIN SPRINGS PETROGLYPHS
John Martin Reservoir, Bent County, Colorado

Site Synopsis

At the end of a dusty, rutted trail, within sight of the John Martin Reservoir, are a series of rock walls with a staggering sequence of petroglyphs. Some are historic—from the 1870s to 1900s—but most are prehistoric. Humanoid figures mesh with arrays of carved dots. The glyphs, some similar to types found elsewhere in Colorado, others unique to the southeast of the state, number in the hundreds.

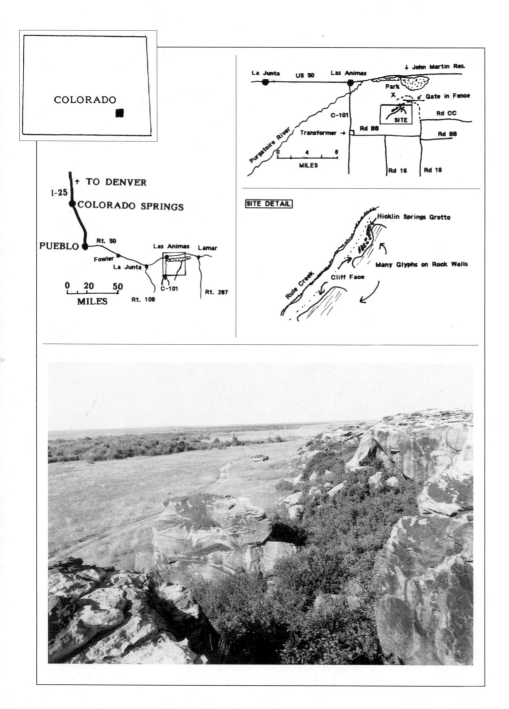

COLORADO

↑ TO DENVER

I-25

COLORADO SPRINGS

Rt. 50

PUEBLO

Fowler

La Junta

Las Animas   Lamar

C-101

Rt. 287

Rt. 109

0   20   50
MILES

La Junta   US 50   Las Animas   ↓ John Martin Res.

Park
X   Gate in Fence

C-101

Transformer →   Rd BB

SITE

Rd CC

Rd BB

Purgatoire River

Rd 16   Rd 18

0   4   8
MILES

SITE DETAIL

Hicklin Springs Grotto

Many Glyphs on Rock Walls

Rule Creek

Cliff Face

This device, of vertical lines intersected by a horizontal line, is found carved on rock walls throughout Colorado. This photograph was taken at the Hicklin Springs site. Some researchers argue that the device is evidence of the use of Ogam, an ancient Celtic writing system, while others claim it is some type of Native American tally system. Note how the rock wall here has cracked, apparently due to the seasonal frost-thaw cycle.

Location

From Denver, take Interstate 25 south to Pueblo. At Pueblo, exit onto Route 50 going east toward La Junta. Drive until you reach Las Animas. Near the center of town, Route 101 will be clearly marked. Travel south on Route 101 for 5.5 miles, turning east (left) onto Road BB. A large electrical transformer is at this turnoff. Travel on Road BB for eight miles until you reach Road 19. Turn north (left) onto Road 19, traveling for one mile. At that point, the road turns to the east (right) onto Road CC. *Do not go onto Road CC.* Before the road veers off to the right, you will see a dirt trail extending from Road 19. Take the trail. Drive *very slowly*

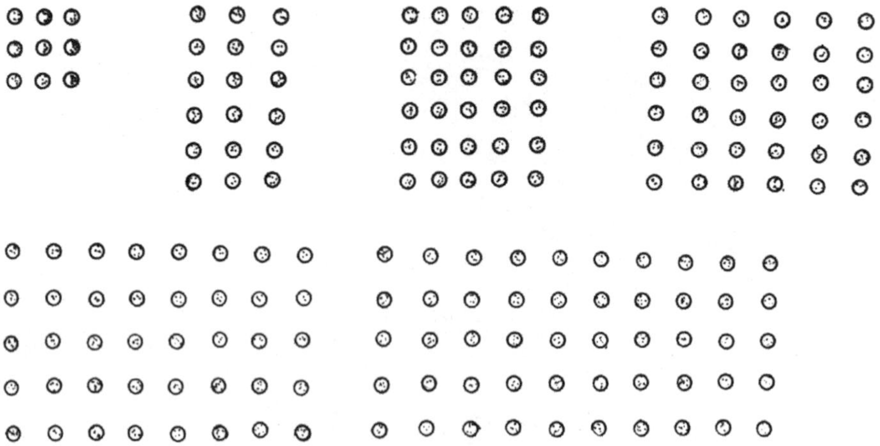

Fig. 2.33. A sketch demonstrating examples of dot matrices found at Hicklin Springs and elsewhere.

because there are many ruts and holes here. Although helpful, a four-wheel-drive vehicle is not mandatory if your car has good clearance and you travel very slowly. Follow this dirt trail for about a mile. It will turn northwest (to the left). Stop at the barbed wire gate. Open the gate (be sure to close it once you drive through!), drive through toward the left. The rock wall faces will quickly come into view. Park anywhere along this trail.

Considerations

Two personal concerns: rattlesnakes and poison ivy. The type of flat rocks that make up this site create the perfect habitat for rather large rattlers. Carry a walking stick with you to tap the ground before walking through grass, vegetation, or between rocks. Also, wear high leather boots and carry a snakebite kit.

Poison ivy is a major problem at Hicklin Springs. It grows right where the best glyphs are. If you visit the site during the summer months—when the ivy and snakes are at their peak—wear long pants, a long-sleeve shirt, and coat your exposed skin with a skin-barrier lotion. This should reduce the chance of getting skin irritation from poison ivy.

One of many pecked dot matrix patterns found at Hicklin Springs and elsewhere throughout southeastern Colorado. Their meaning is unknown to modern researchers.

The best advice is to go in early spring or late autumn—either before the ivy sprouts and when the snakes are still sluggish or when the ivy leaves die and the snakes slow down due to the colder nights.

History/Background

Flood control is a serious concern along the Arkansas River. As one travels east from Pueblo to Las Animas, it is easy to understand why: Most of the farms and business related to agriculture are located along the river's floodplain. Levees line both banks of the river along this route.

A number of years ago the Army Corp of Engineers was assigned the task of building a reservoir to better maintain floodwater. Within a few years levees were shored up and the John Martin Reservoir was constructed to help control any potential overspill. The Hicklin Springs site is currently under the domain of the Army Corp of Engineers—a federal agency. It is therefore open to public usage (no locks can be put on the barbed wire gate leading to the site). In fact, if you ever do find the gate locked, simply contact the sheriff's office in Las Animas. It will be opened for you. The fish and game division of the state of Colorado oversees the site from Denver.

During a recent field trip to Hicklin Springs, student researchers Margaret Hoover and Anna Cayton-Holland noticed a number of peculiar patterns to the glyphs. They found a matrix of pecked dots in various configurations (see Figure 2.33). A recurring pattern was found at the site. The pecked holes clustered into groups of nine (three by three), eighteen (three by six), thirty (five by six), thirty-six (six by six), forty (five by eight), and fifty (five by ten).

The Hicklin Springs site is impressive due to the large number of carvings found in a small area. Within a quarter-mile stretch of rock there are hundreds of carvings of unknown origin and meaning.

Walk beyond the main rock face to the end of the dirt trail toward a dried streambed. Along this arroyo on the sheer walls of the bedrock are hundreds of carvings: spirals, rows of dots, and painted humanlike figures. The region is isolated, barren, and starkly beautiful. Climb atop one of the ridges and think about the activity that once took place there. Try to imagine the meaning of the symbols all around you.

Contact Persons and Organizations

Bill McGlone
La Junta, CO 81050

Colorado Historical Society
Office of Archeological and Historic Preservation
1300 Broadway
Denver, CO 80203-2137
(303) 866-3395

Colorado Division of Wildlife
6060 Broadway
Denver, CO 80216

Southwestern Colorado

Southwestern Colorado is relatively flat country. Over the eons, various rivers have carved out long and deep canyons along the western slope of the Continental Divide, exposing nearly horizontal beds of ancient rock. Due to the scant moisture in the region, the vegetation is sparse and gives the appearance of a semidesert. Yet the report of an early explorer makes clear the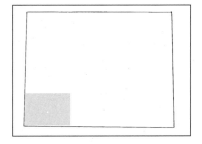
obvious—with a decidedly nineteenth-century racist attitude toward the Indian: "...there is bountiful evidence that at one time it supported a numerous population; there is scarcely a square mile in the 6,000 examined that does not furnish evidence of previous occupation by a race totally distinct from the nomadic savages who hold it now and in many ways superior to them."[5]

Southwestern Colorado is loaded with ruins. In the early 1900s the region around one of the most famous—Mesa Verde—but by all means not the only one of its type, was made into a national park. Throughout the years, the National Park Service, out of necessity, has made a trip there both fascinating yet surprisingly sterile. Yes, the structures are still in place, but there are ladders and guidebooks that attempt to explain the sacred in functional terms. Furthermore, the large numbers of people visiting the site—especially during the summer months—makes for a frantic, rushed visit. Stay away from this national park until the fall or winter months, when the place is virtually deserted. Contact Mesa Verde National Park, CO 81330, (303) 529-4461.

Since the early days of exploration, much emphasis has been placed by archeologists on examining and explaining the multitude of mysterious structures in this area (see Figure 2.34). There are several very good guidebooks whose information will not be duplicated here. One of the best is David Grant Noble's *Ancient Ruins of the Southwest*. In this book, Noble lists the latest information on the structures. He also gives practical hints and advice for those who want to experience the ancient ones.

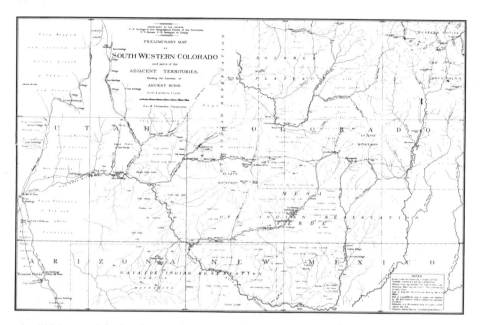

An 1876 map of the Southwest, showing the locations of ancient ruins. (Reprinted from Hayden, *Tenth Annual Report*)

Cliff House, in the Canon of the Mancos, southwestern Colorado. (Reprinted from Hayden, *Tenth Annual Report*)

Right: *Cliff Fortress, in southwestern Colorado—southeastern Utah.* (Reprinted from Hayden, *Tenth Annual Report*)

Bottom: *A view of the plan of Spruce Tree House at Mesa Verde, in southwestern Colorado.*

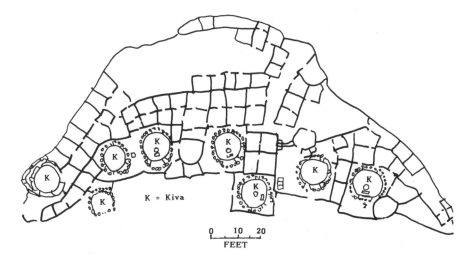

K = Kiva

0   10   20
FEET

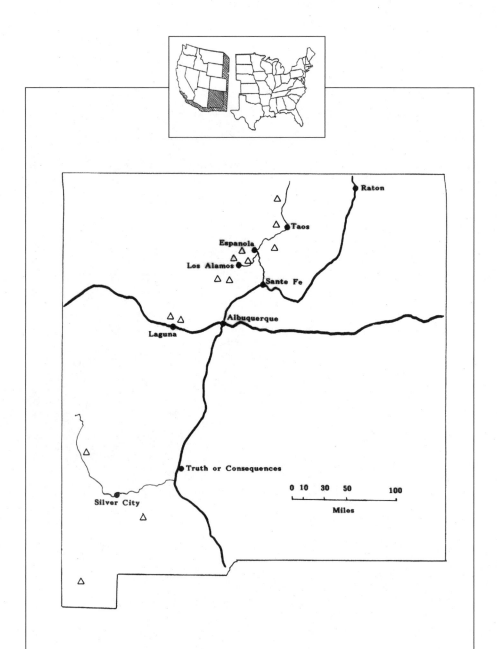

Mysterious Sites in New Mexico

3

New Mexico

New Mexico is littered with mysterious sites. Its geology alone—the product of volcanic catastrophe, millennia of wind and water erosion, and a continent-size rift pulling the state apart—allows for some weird scenery.

The ancient ruins in the state are overwhelming. There are thousands of cliff dwelling and pueblo sites scattered throughout this spectacular region. Edgar L. Hewett, an early twentieth-century Sante Fe archeologist, described it best:

> If you want to feel the power and pathos of time, roll up in your blanket some night on any one of a hundred mesas, or in any one of a hundred canyons of the old abandoned land of the Pajaritans [the region around Espanola-Los Alamos]. The stars that sparkle down on you watched over the cataclysm that rent the nearby mountains some millions of years ago; saw the vast blanket of volcanic ash laid down around the yawning crater, the largest on the world's surface; saw the mesas rise out of the chaos, the rifts deepened into gorges; saw vegetation again creep over the ashen landscape, forests slowly wrap the mountain sides in green, and wild life seek timidly the shelter of aspen and pine; saw cliffs and caves shaped by wind and rain; and, at last, saw human life drift quietly in, take up the routine of orderly existence, then quietly flow on into the ocean which we call Time. Listen to the winds that sang through the pines a thousand years ago—melodies that, unknown and unnoticed through silent centuries, have never ceased and never will.[1]

An engraving of the badlands of New Mexico. (Reprinted from Winchell, *Geological Excursions*, author's collection)

Hewett traveled the ancient trails of northern New Mexico in the late 1890s, "...when the stillness and the mystery of it were undisturbed." Forty years after his original explorations, he assembled his notes and papers into a handbook of archeological history. But this early explorer sensed something that still haunts visitors today: "I am sensible of the futility of a book about a place where all realities have melted into shadows. Who can describe silence and space and time, and a world of only immemorial spirits? ...Indians know all about it, but are too wise to try to utter it."[2]

New Mexico is a land where one occasionally glimpses the shadows of time past. The violence of volcanic upheaval becomes evident when hiking through a canyon. Other times, glimpses of what the region must have looked like a thousand years ago become clear: crisp mountain streams, green floodplains, vast numbers of people scurrying about high mesas: laughter, song, dance. The silence of the high-canyon cliff dwellings today is in direct contrast to what once was. Listen carefully to the wind. The primeval song of the earth and the ancient voice of human spirits abound in this mysterious locale.

Northwestern New Mexico

Northwestern New Mexico was first explored for its mineral potential and overland route possibilities back in the early nineteenth century by army lieutenant J. H. Simpson. By the 1870s, geologist William H. Holmes and photographer William H. Jackson were the first researchers to systematically survey southwestern Colorado's and northwestern New Mexico's staggering number of archeological remains. The ruins in and around Chaco Canyon surprised everyone because of their massiveness and grandeur. Pueblo Bonito, a massive stone apartment complex where up to sixty thousand people once lived, was the focus of much early debate. Some scholars believed the structure was built by Mexican Aztecs, while others erroneously assumed an extinct white race were the architects. Today we know that all of the remains in and around Chaco Canyon were built by a mysterious people called by the Navajo *Anasazi*, "The Ancient Ones."

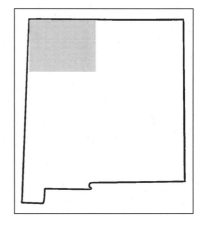

The area is now home to several large Indian reservations. The most impressive set of ruins are those on the Ute Reservation. Most people visiting southwestern Colorado's Four Corners region opt to go to Mesa Verde for a day trip. The Ute Reservation, however, is much less traveled. Four-wheel-drive and a guided tour throughout this staggering region will get one closer to what Lieutenant Simpson saw almost 150 years ago.

1849 SIMPSON EXPEDITION
Northwest New Mexico, Northeast Arizona

Site Synopsis

The first expedition to accurately map the region of northwest

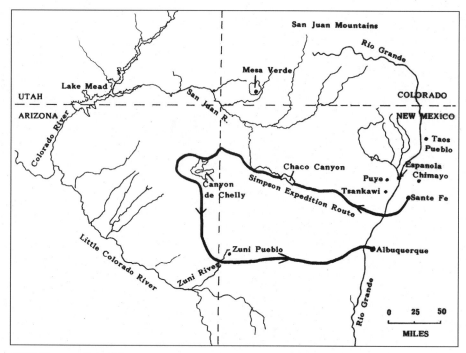

1849 Simpson Expedition

New Mexico was led in by U.S. Army Lieutenant J. H. Simpson in 1849. Simpson tagged along with Lieutenant Colonel John M. Washington, who held the dual roles of chief of the 9th military department as well as governor of New Mexico. Simpson and a troop of four hundred men spent two months marching into what was then known as "Navajo Country." Washington's mission was to extract a peace treaty with the Navajo to insure that settlers moving west from the Rio Grande to the Pacific Coast wouldn't be harmed. Simpson, an engineer in the government's Bureau of Topography, had the responsibility of describing the geology of the route. Two artists assisted on the journey: R. H. Kern sketched the geology and the ruin sites, while his brother, E. M. Kern, concentrated on drawing an accurate topographic map of the region.

History/Background

Simpson and the army troops marched southwest from Santa Fe for sixteen miles before traveling west over the Jemez Mountains and into the region today known as Chaco Canyon. They rode on horseback with wagons, averaging around twenty miles per day between camps. In total, they covered over one thousand miles during August and September, exploring a region that few had the courage (or military might) to enter for extended periods of time.

The landscape astonished and surprised the young lieutenant:

The idea I...adhered to...before ever having seen this country, was that...it was also like the country of the States, generally fertile and covered with verdure. But never did I have, nor do I believe anybody can have a full appreciation of the almost universal barrenness which pervades this country until they come out as I did to "search the land," and behold with their own eyes its general nakedness. The primary mountains...are usually of a rounded form covered by a dull, lifeless-colored soil and generally destitute of any other sylva than pine and cedar, most frequently of a sparse and dwarfish character. The face of the country...has a tendency to create...a sensation of loathing.[3]

Nonetheless, in reading through Simpson's report one is struck by the eagerness of the lieutenant to seek out various ruins he clearly had heard about. He makes reference to several earlier preliminary expeditions into the region that described fanciful water springs or "ruins" of adobe, not stone. In many cases, Simpson tactfully debunks earlier bits of misinformation.

When near a potential site based on information supplied by his Mexican-Indian guide, Simpson would always ask for permission to leave the cavalry. Upon receiving it, Simpson, Kern, and the guide would ride out on horseback for a few days of exploration before trying to catch up to the continually advancing cavalry. Limited time was always a problem when investigating an ancient site. As Simpson put it: "We would gladly, had time permitted, have remained longer to dig among the rubbish of the past; but the troops having already got some miles in advance of us, we were reluctantly obliged to quit"[4]

The journey is remarkable, for it not only accurately details the geology of the region for the first time, but it also describes poignant episodes between white and Indian cultures that must have happened dozens of times in the settlement of the West. Simpson writes about a conversation with an Indian from the Jemez Pueblo.

> I asked him whether they [the Pueblo Indians] now looked upon God and the sun as the same being. He said they did. The question was then put, whether they still worshipped the sun, as God, with contrition of the heart. His reply was, "Why not? He governs the world!"
>
> From this Indian I also learned that they worship the sun with most pleasure in the morning, and they have priests to administer their own religion, which they like better than the Roman Catholic, which he says has been forced upon them, and which they do not understand. [5]

He also describes a part of New Mexico that is long gone. Twelve miles from Alberquerque, the troops stopped at Algadones for the night.

> This miserable-looking village contains about forty houses and has a population of some two or three hundred souls. ... The inn, kept by a Mexican, is far from being such as it should be, either as respects cleanliness or the character of the *cuisine*. Miserably muddy coffee, a stew made of mutton smothered in onions, half-baked *tortillas*, and a few boiled eggs, constitute the best meal it pretends to furnish. I do not know why it is, but I have not yet drunk a cup of coffee or eaten a *tortilla* of Mexican preparation without its creating...a sensation of nausea...There is certainly room for improvement in the *cuisine* of this country. [6]

There is a sense of humor that is usually lacking in reports of this type: "Having by a few moments experience, last evening, become convinced that if I lay within doors all night I should not only have a fight with rabid insects, but have also great violence done to my *olfactories*, Lieutenant Ward and myself slept in the wagon; and a pretty comfortable night we have had of it."[7]

Simpson and his two companions were amazed by the ruins they saw. They were also frustrated that no one among the Indians knew anything about them. "In regard to the origin of these remains," he writes, "there is nothing that I can learn conclusive in relation to it."[8] Simpson even reported asking the governor of the Zuni Pueblo about the cliffside ruins. The Governor "says he has seen them, but knows nothing of their origin."[9]

As one reads the report, Simpson's admiration of the mysterious people who built the structures becomes clear. Its conclusions also contributed to the bizarre theories about a vanished pre-Indian civilization inhabiting early America:

> The ruins...are evidently from the similarity of their style and mode of construction, of a common origin; they discover in the materials of which they are composed, as well as in the grandeur of their design and superiority of their workmanship, a condition of architectural excellence beyond the power of the Indians or New Mexicans of the present day to exhibit.... these remains discover a race of men superior to the natives of New Mexico of the present day.[10]

The artist Kern produced several on-the-spot sketches of the geology, archeology, and Pueblo Indians he met along the way. These sketches, often done, in his own words, on poor-quality paper, were later made into lithographs included in Simpson's report. They capture the wildness and mystery of the region.

Exploring the ruins of the area today, especially some of the less-traveled routes, might bring to mind Lieutenant Simpson's September 18, 1849, journal entry:

> The excitement of yesterday's discovery, together with a rather hard pallet, and the howling wolves, prevented my having as comfortable night's rest as I would have liked. Often did I gaze, in my restlessness...to witness the culmination of that beautiful constellation, Orion, the precursor, at this season of the year, of

Fig. 3.1. An engraving of a natural sandstone column in northwestern New Mexico. (Reprinted from Johnston, Reports of the Secretary of War with Reconnaissance of Routes from San Antonio to El Paso, author's collection)

the approach of day, and as often did I find myself obliged to exercise that most difficult of virtues, patience—the sure key, with proper application...to success.[11]

A sample of the lithographs accompanying Lieutenant Simpson's report attest to the strange and weird countryside he rode through (see Figures 3.1 and 3.2).

Fig. 3.2. An engraving of the entrance to Canyon de Chelly, a region filled with spectacular ruins. (Reprinted from Johnston, Reports)

Contact Persons and Organizations

One of the most knowledgeable persons on the early expeditions to the Southwest is George Robinson, owner of G. Robinson's Old Prints and Maps in Taos, New Mexico. Mr. Robinson is an expert on the minutiae of these and other expeditions. He also has an impressive collection of maps and prints from this expedition and others for sale. His store is located at 124-D Bent Street, Taos, N.M. 87571; (505) 758-2278. Fax: (505) 758-1606.

The Western History Collection of the Denver Public Library is also one of the better sources to see these reports firsthand, as is the University of Colorado at Boulder, which was and still is a repository for government publications.

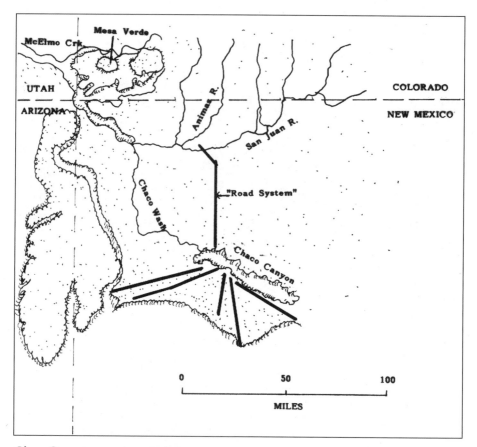

Chaco Canyon mysterious roads

CHACO CANYON'S MYSTERIOUS ROADS
Chaco Canyon National Park, New Mexico

Site Synopsis

Radiating out from the twelfth-century Anasazi site of Chaco Canyon like the spokes of a wheel are numerous "roads" that spread outward in straight lines, some of which extend forty to sixty miles. These enigmatic boulevards are shallow depressions thirty to forty feet wide and sometimes lined with stones. There is no evidence that they were ever used by the Anasazi as transport mediums for trade or anything else. Furthermore, these pathways move in direct alignment regardless of any surface feature like hills, valleys, or rocks—they move over, under, and through them with total disregard for the blocking structure.

All indications suggest that these roads were part of a long-forgotten cosmology of the ancient Anasazi. There are some intriguing similarities, however, to recently understood lines found elsewhere in the Americas.

Location

Chaco Canyon is part of the Chaco Culture National Historical Park in northwestern New Mexico. From Sante Fe, take I-25 south for approximately forty miles, turning northwest on Route 44. Travel on Route 44, passing through the Jemez Indian Reservation, the town of Cuba, and Counselor before reaching Blanco (approximately 120 miles). At Blanco, turn south on Route 57 for twenty-three miles. Drive up to the park headquarters for site maps and further information.

Considerations

Chaco Canyon is part of the National Parks system. Camping is permitted only in specified regions of the park. As a federal site, all artifact hunting and collecting is strictly prohibited here. If you see something ancient sticking out of the ground, leave it there and tell a park ranger. It may be just the key that future archeologists need to figure out this overwhelming puzzle.

Bring plenty of food and water. If camping, bring appropriate seasonal gear. Many of the sites demand a good day's hike. The road system demands a trek of several days.

History/Background

There are many interesting features in the Chaco Canyon region: great kivas, ruined pueblos, cliffside caves, petroglyphs, and thousands of shards of pottery strewn about the land like decoration.

The Simpson and Jackson-Holmes expeditions to this region, in 1849 and in the 1870s, set the stage for future research. They left us with fascinating early surveys and descriptions of the structures within the canyon (see page 000).

Chaco Canyon was the center of a great Anasazi cultural complex. By A.D. 1115, several spectacular pueblos were constructed within the canyon, such as Pueblo Bonito, an eight-hundred-room site with extraordinary stone masonry and many kivas. Furthermore, by this time there were hundreds of outlying pueblos with seeming connections to Chaco Canyon. Many of these outlying sites are connected by the mysterious road system.

Researchers in the 1920s and 1930s assumed the roads radiating out from the canyon were merely for transport. It wasn't until the 1950s and 1960s, when accurately drawn surveys plotted them out with meticulous care, that the strange nature of these pathways

Fig. 3.3. Engraving of an ancient stairway carved into the canyon wall behind Pueblo Bonito, in Chaco Canyon. The cut stairs lead to an ancient "road." (Reprinted from Johnston, Reports)

became obvious. The pathways move onward for miles with apparent disregard for hills, mesas, streams, and other natural features. They are perplexing, for where in many cases it would have been easier to go around a hilltop feature, the road will go over it via hand-cut stairways (see Figure 3.3). Transport roads they were not, for easier trails around some of the obstacles exist. By A.D. 1200,

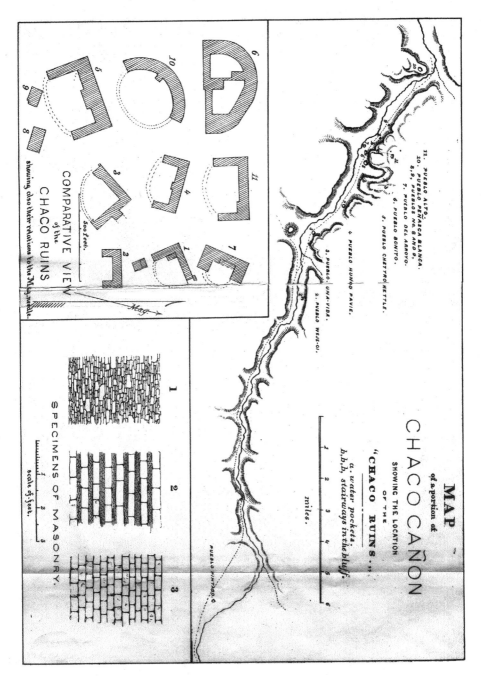

An 1876 map of Chaco Canyon. (Reprinted from Hayden, *Tenth Annual Report*)

Chaco Canyon, the outlying pueblos, and the roads were abandoned, no doubt due to extreme drought conditions as indicated in
tree-ring analysis of pueblo wood beams.

The question remains, What were the roads built for? This is
difficult to answer positively. However, by examining other places
in the world where living cultures have constructed similar "cosmic" pathways, we may shed light on the mind-set of the Ancient
Ones at Chaco Canyon.

The Kogi Indians of northern Colombia have an astonishing
cosmology. Crisscrossing their high sierra territory are mysterious
pathways that link ancient towns, run up rivers, disappear beneath
buildings, and continue onward in absolutely straight lines. These
mysterious landscape lines relate to the travels of spirits.[12] There is
a spiritual geography within the community that's manifest in the
carved pathways emanating from the villages. The gravel-stone
roadways are sacred places that must be walked and maintained if
one is to please the spirits.

The physical roads move outwards and blend with the spiritual. People walking along the pathways move onto higher levels
of consciousness by the act of walking. Maintaining harmony in
the Kogi world is done by keeping the roads. Scattered around the
roads are places where communication with the spirit world takes
place, These places include ruined archeological sites, large boulders, streams and hillsides.The Kogi believe that the physical and
spiritual worlds coexist and that actions taking place in one world
are also expressed in the other world. As a result of this cosmologi-
cal "linkage," the Kogi have a deep awareness and respect of their
natural surroundings. They are intimately in tune with the earth—
they have to be, for the spirit world exists in and around their
physical world.

The ancient people of Chaco Canyon in northwestern New
Mexico probably used their roads in a similar way to the Kogi. The
physical parallels are numerous. Countless petroglyph sites along
the way also suggest that messages were being relayed to the physical and, perhaps, the spiritual world as well.

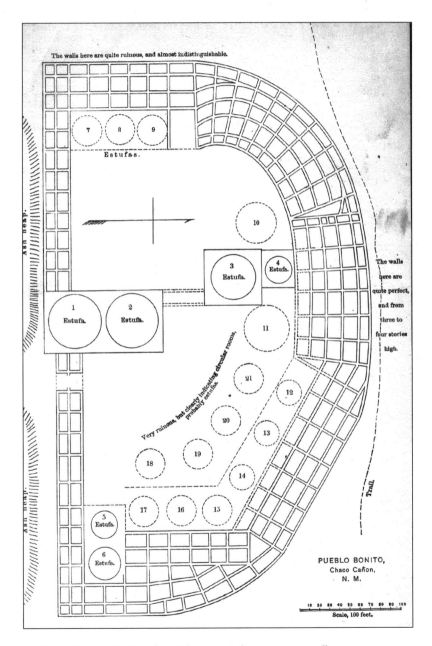

A plan of Pueblo Bonito, one of the region's largest ancient village sites.
(Reprinted from Hayden, *Tenth Annual Report*)

Contact Persons and Organizations

Chaco Culture Historical Park
Star Route 4, Box 6500
Bloomfield, N.M. 87413

North-Central New Mexico

Northern New Mexico is defined by ancient volcanic activity. The ancient cliff dwellers as well as people living there now adapted in direct proportion to the actions of geological processes that happened a long time ago.

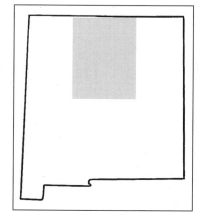

Over a million years ago, a vast volcano exploded, sending billions of tons of ash and debris out over the land. In time this volcanic material solidified into a material collectively known as *tuff*. The volcanic crater collapsed upon itself, and, later, lava domes bubbled up, obscuring the true ringlike pattern of this sixteen-mile-wide plugged volcano opening. Today the extinct crater outline can only be appreciated from satellite images. In fact, in the 1930s, geologists were still arguing whether this area was actually a crater. It is. From the ground the peaked rim of the eroded crater is collectively known as the Jemez Mountains. The interior of the collapsed opening is known as the Vallez Caldera.

The entire region of central New Mexico is sitting in the midst of two continent-sized plates that are pulling apart (see Figure 3.4). Any place where such plates meet exposes giant cracks in the earth's surface. This allows magma—liquid rock—deep within the crust to move toward the surface. Volcanoes are the surface manifestation of deep stresses and geological chaos within the earth.

The volcanic ash that exploded onto the region—in some places it is over two thousand feet thick—eroded into high walled canyons as thousands of years of rain, wind, and snow carved their way into the soft rock. Natural cavities in the rock were caused by volcanic gasses escaping from the slowly cooling ash. Tribes of Native Americans found their way to this place over two thousand years ago and settled along the canyons. South-facing cliffside

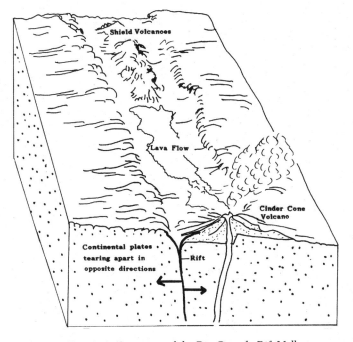

Fig. 3.4. Anatomy of the Rio Grande Rift Valley.

caves were carved along the high canyon walls. Later in time, on the mesa tops communal pueblos were constructed out of the soft rock.

As one travels throughout all of New Mexico, the evidence of a once-vast population living among the canyons, mesa tops, and floodplains is everywhere in the form of pottery shards, stone slabs, and pueblo ruins.

RIO GRANDE RIFT
Wild Rivers Recreation Area, Questa and Taos, New Mexico

Site Synopsis

Thirty million years ago the Rio Grande Rift was created by a pulling apart of the earth's crust. Deep within the earth, two gigantic "bubbles" in the mantle may have caused a slow rolling apart

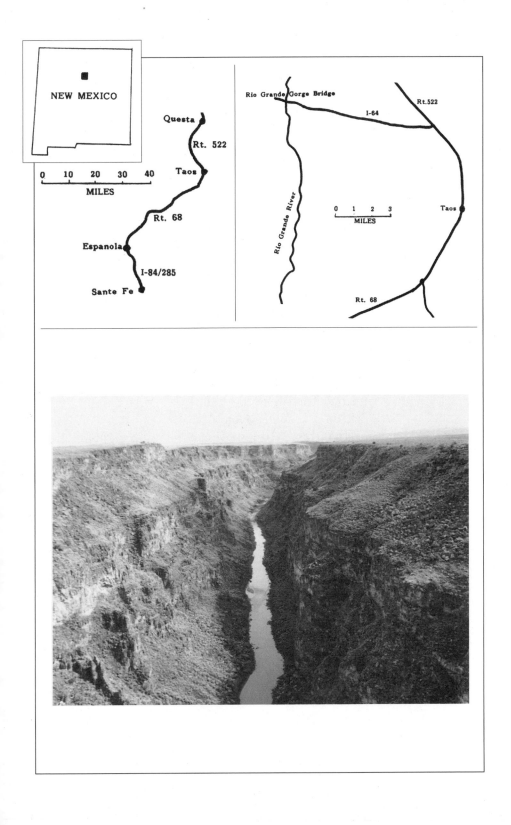

similar to the geological mechanism at work along midoceanic ridges. If this is so, visitors to this rift may be seeing the very beginning of a new ocean basin!

Location

Travel south on Route 522 from San Luis, Colorado. Before the town of Questa there is a turnoff (west on Route 378) leading to the Wild Rivers Recreation Area. Drive down this road for seven miles, stopping occasionally at the various rest-scenic views. At the end of the road is a ranger station. Park here and walk a few hundred yards to the viewing spot. The scene is staggering. A yawning canyon opens out into space. This is the confluence of the Red and Rio Grande Rivers.

There are several hiking areas leading down to the rivers. Give yourself at least an hour and a half for the trek down and two hours for the hike back up to the road.

After leaving the Wild Rivers Area, proceed south on Route 522 toward Taos. Just before the town is a blinking light. Turn right toward the Rio Grande Gorge (the airport is also along this road). In about seven miles pull off at the rest area and walk over the bridge. Be prepared to have your breath taken away.

Considerations

Hiking down to the Rio Grande at the Wild Rivers region is slow going and dangerous, especially if it is raining. Be wary of afternoon lightning and thunderstorms. If you get caught while hiking, take immediate cover. Trails are steep and hiking can be strenuous. Carry lots of water.

Camping is allowed only in designated campsites along and below the rim. Campsites along the river require a hike in.

The Wild Rivers Recreation Area has been set aside to allow the public to enjoy the Red and Rio Grande Rivers. The area is protected under the Wild and Scenic Rivers Act of 1968. At this site, both rivers are preserved in their natural, free-flowing states. (See Figure 3.5.)

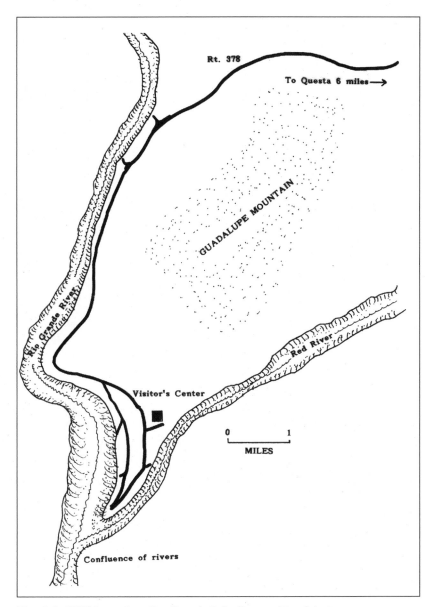

Fig. 3.5. Wild River Area Rio Grande Rift, Questa, New Mexico.

History/Background

Understanding the Rio Grande Rift puts all of New Mexico's geological and archeological anomalies into perspective. It allows for a framework by which to comprehend the complexities of the land and the ancient people who lived there. This is a very powerful place. It forces one to face the true antiquity of our planet.

The Rio Grande Gorge Bridge, towering over six hundred feet above the river just outside of Taos, New Mexico, offers a midrift view. There are pedestrian walkways along both sides of the bridge. Be forewarned: When trucks pass over the bridge it vibrates heavily.

The Rio Grande Rift exists because two continent-sized plates are ripping the state apart. They have been separating and widening for several million years, and they will continue to do so. (See Figure 3.6.)

Wherever continental plates come together there are volcanoes. Volcanoes are gigantic cracks in the earth where liquid rock rises to the surface and escapes. The Taos volcanic plateau contains many cinder-cone and shield volcanoes. Cinder-cone volcanoes are steep-sloped mounds made up of solidified ash and other pyroclastic debris. Magma usually erupts out of the cone with explosive force. Shield volcanoes are large rounded mounds. Magma usually slowly oozes out of this type of volcano. Several exist in the Taos plateau with clear evidence of ancient lava flows.

When lava cools slowly, it forms distinctive columns. These are clearly evident at the Rio Grande Gorge Bridge. When looking at these dark black palisades of rock, think of the enormous amount of fiery rock that spewed out of the earth's depths, layering and filling the plateau over and over until it reached the height we see today. The Rio Grande Rift would be close to thirty thousand feet deep and would be filled with Gulf of Mexico seawater if it had not been filled up with the billions of tons of lava, gravel, and ash from the scores of volcanoes within the plateau.

The Rift is intriguing because it cuts down to the mantle of the earth. It opens up the ground like a wound tearing into the crust. Places like this have always inspired people who are sensitive to earth energy forces. Taos is no different. In fact, Taos has been attracting artists and writers to the region since the early 1900s,

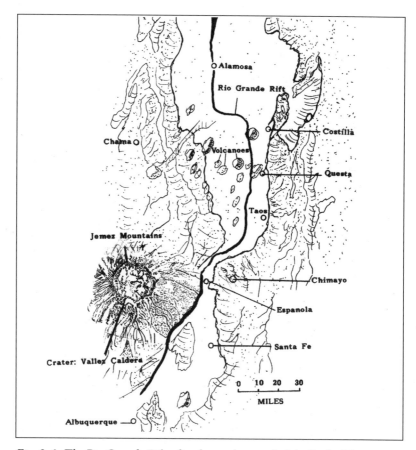

Fig. 3.6. The Rio Grande Rift splits the southern end of the Rocky Mountains into the Sangre de Cristo Range of the east and the Tusas and Brazos Mountains to the west.

when the first came "because of the light." Perhaps it was something more. Why do so many ancient pueblos line the Rift? Why is the Taos Pueblo located where it is—within eight miles of the Rift and a few miles from the mountains?

The region around this gap in the earth's crust is best appreciated at night. Drive to the bridge or take one of the many roads (Road 567, for example) that lead to the Rift edge. Experience how this yawning chasm overwhelms the senses, particularly if the moon is out.

Recently, some of the residents of Taos have been experiencing an annoying humming sound. Residents describe it as a low-frequency background hum similar to the sound of a distant idling diesel engine. At first thought to be something specific to a few overly sensitive individuals—perhaps people with a hearing defect— research teams from the University of New Mexico spent several weeks in the Taos area armed with sophisticated sound-recording equipment. They concluded that the residents were in fact hearing a humming sound that was not imagined but real and distinct. The only problem was that the scientists could not determine where the sound was coming from or what was causing it. The hum seemed to be coming from all directions. It was impossible to pinpoint the source because there wasn't any specific site to point to as the source. The University of New Mexico has allocated $37,000 to survey residents in an attempt to locate the source of the mysterious hum.

There are two possible explanations. The first is that the hum has something to do with government experimentation at the Los Alamos Laboratories—a site some forty-five miles south of Taos. Some Taos residents believe the hum has something to do with secret military weaponry. Perhaps; the Los Alamos facility started out as a supersecret lab during World War II. Its mission was to develop an atomic bomb.

The second explanation deals with less easily accepted concepts. Is it possible that the giant rips in the earth's crust caused by the unimaginable pressure of deep rocky plates rubbing and mashing against one another is somehow responsible for this hum? If so, is it a portent of more volcanic activity? Central New Mexico experiences frequent earthquakes. This makes perfect sense as the massive blocks of crust slip, slide, and slam against one another.

The Taos hum is one manifestation of the mysterious energy associated with the Rio Grande Rift.

Contact Persons and Organizations

The Art Zimmerman Visitor Center at the Wild Rivers Recreation Area is open every day from Memorial Day weekend through Labor Day weekend from 9:00 A.M. to 5:00 P.M.

POT CREEK CULTURAL SITE
Carson National Forest, south of Taos, New Mexico

Site Synopsis

Six miles south of Taos along the old high-road mountain trail to Sante Fe is part of the largest pueblo ruin in northern New Mexico. Built in the thirteenth century by the Anasazi, it was inhabited for 150 years before being abandoned. Why did the ancient people who lived here settle so far up in the mountains? Why did they leave?

Location

Travel four miles south of Taos center, turning south on Route 518. In six miles you will see the entrance to the Pot Creek Cultural Site. One-half mile beyond the gate is Southern Methodist University's refurbished Fort Burgwin Research Center.

Considerations

Please respect the land and leave all artifacts in place.

Permission to visit the main Pot Creek Pueblo must be obtained from the SMU Fort Burgwin Research Center before entering the dig site. The best time to visit is during the summer field school, when teams of students are actively engaged in unraveling this site's intriguing past.

History/Background

When visiting this site, forget the U.S. Forest Service–issue picnic tables, look past the gravel trail, and focus on the surrounding hilltops, where one thousand years ago this high-plateau valley was teeming with life. This is a spiritual place—the ancestral home of the Taos and Picuris Pueblos.

For over one thousand years the land in this area has been

continually settled. There's good archeological data to prove this. But people had been coming onto this land for thousands of years longer. Not too far outside the Taos and Rio Grande area there's evidence that hunters as early as seven thousand years ago camped and hunted while searching for animals who came to drink.

Pot Creek gets its name from the enormous number of Indian ceramic vessels found along the streambed over the last several hundred years. The Pot Creek people were Anasazi Indians who migrated east into the Rio Grande from the Chaco Canyon region of New Mexico, over one thousand years ago. These people farmed the land, dug ditches for irrigation, and terraced the mountainsides.

The gravel trail constructed by the Forest Service guides one along a path past a kiva and reconstructed pueblo. Along the way there are piñon trees and examples of land-leveling techniques. What you see here is a tiny example of what lies beyond the trees. Due east of here, beyond the barbed wire fence, is the largest pueblo site in northern New Mexico. Currently under excavation by Southern Methodist University workers housed at Fort Burgwin, the Pot Creek Pueblo is suspected of having over eight hundred apartment-style rooms! How did all those people live together? How did they get enough to eat?

Fort Burgwin lay buried and unnoticed for more than one hundred years. Named for Captain John Burgwin, commander of the First Dragoons, who was killed in an early New Mexican battle, the complex was built in 1852 as a temporary fort to protect the main wagon road between Taos and Sante Fe from the marauding Comanche and Apache. By the early 1860s, as need for protection diminished and U.S. troops were needed to fight the Civil War, the fort was abandoned. In the mid-1950s, an amateur archeologist found the remains of the fort and convinced Southern Methodist University to establish a research center on the site. The fort was rebuilt based on early drawings of the site. A field school was established to excavate the Pot Creek Pueblo.

The people who lived at Pot Creek thrived, as indicated by the large number of ruins and giant kivas now undergoing excavation. The ancient potters developed a black-line-on-white-background glaze that is beautiful. The many complete pots excavated at this location attest to the artistic skill these people possessed.

When walking through the area, it is easy to understand its attraction. Located at an altitude of 7,400 feet in a valley of the Sangre de Cristo Mountains, the pueblo sits near the junction of two streams. It is a beautiful, peaceful setting with a constant source of water. The mountain altitude allowed early people to exploit food ecosystems both at higher and lower elevations—nuts, berries, piñon seeds, and game. But with altitude there are problems, most significantly the very short growing season. How these people managed to live in the region for over 150 years on such short seasonal food availability is unknown. However, the reason for their leaving may have an answer in the pots.

Pottery was an essential craft to the early Anasazi. At the primary level, pottery allowed them to transport water and store seeds for seasonal plantings. But making pottery demands high heat: To reach the temperatures necessary to fire clay requires a lot of wood. Perhaps it took 150 years to thoroughly deplete the surrounding mountainsides of the fuel necessary to continue making a commodity essential to the pueblo's existence? Archeologists do know that by the mid- to late 1300s the Pot Creek Pueblo site was abandoned. Soon afterwards, the Picuris and Taos Pueblos were formed.

Walk the grounds of this site and capture the magical experience of feeling at one with the surroundings. No doubt this spot was chosen as a pueblo site not only because of the presence of water, but also because it felt right.

Contact Persons and Organizations

Fort Burgwin
Route 518
Taos, N.M. 87571
(505) 758-8322

Or contact: Southern Methodist University
SMU-IN-TAOS Office, Room 108 Boaz Hall West
Southern Methodist University, Dallas, TX 75275
(214) 768-3657

SACRED EARTH
Chimayo, New Mexico

Site Synopsis

In a mountain town in north-central New Mexico, near two fast-moving streams at the base of a majestic peak sits a small church known as El Sanctuario de Chimayo (The Sanctuary of Chimayo). In the floor of a small room next to the church's altar is a hole packed with mud. Each year, thousands of people make pilgrimages to this room to pray and to rub themselves with the moist earth, hoping for physical and spiritual relief. In an adjacent room hang scores of crutches, braces, and photos left by people who claim to have been miraculously cured of their ailments by the sacred earth. Investigation into this site reveals that it was a place of great power long before Spanish colonists settled the Chimayo Valley. Tewa Indians (a culturally and linguistically distinct tribe that currently inhabits the many Pueblos along the Rio Grande) worshipped at this very spot, using the healing mud for centuries. Why?

Location

From Sante Fe, travel north on I-25 for twenty-four miles. At Española turn northeast on Road 76. Chimayo is ten miles up this road. Once in the town, follow the signs leading to the sanctuary.

Considerations

The Sanctuary of Chimayo is a fully operating Catholic church. People go there to pray and to attend daily Mass. The church and various side rooms are filled with statues and paintings of saints. The rituals associated with the healing power of the mud are steeped in Catholic tradition. Most worshippers at Chimayo are not aware of the true antiquity and Native American origins of the site. They assume it is a Christian-based, miraculous place, comparable to Lourdes in France. Although they are wrong, respect for their perspective is advised.

Most of the people who visit the church are in some degree of

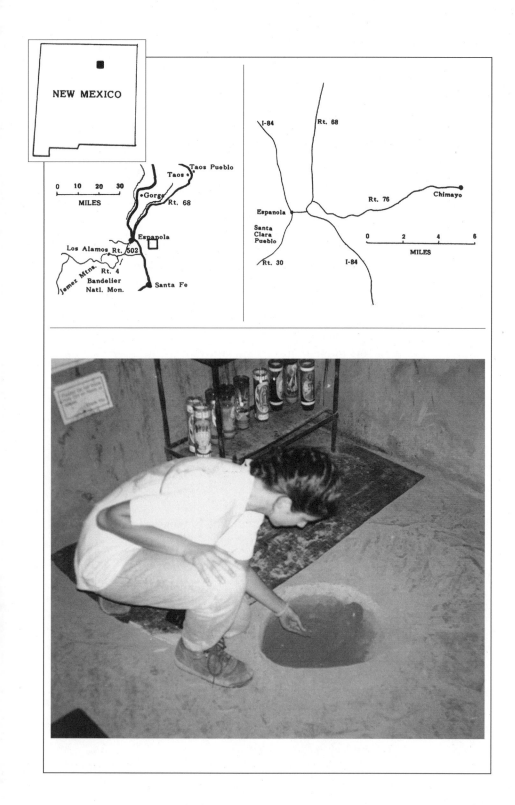

emotional or physical pain. There is perhaps more sorrow than joy at this site. One morning, a woman with a two-month-old baby walked into the room. The baby was attached to a portable oxygen respirator. The woman knelt down, dabbed the baby with earth, and wept.

History/Background

The Sanctuario is wrought with obscure and conflicting legends. In the 1950s, anthropologist Stephen Borhegyi did some of the original research to sort out the various stories. Borhegyi discovered the Sanctuario had many parallels with a little-known church in Central America. In the town of Esquipulas, Guatemala, there's a tradition of healing earth associated with a rather specialized carving of a wooden crucifix. Chimayo has an almost identical copy of the Esquipulas crucifix. Borhegyi's research suggests that sometime in the early 1800s a resident of Chimayo either traveled to or heard firsthand of the Esquipulas shrine. In 1818, a petition to build a church at Chimayo was granted. Scholarly opinion is that the church incorporated a very ancient Indian site. Pottery dating to A.D. 1100, as well as the finding of hand-worked obsidian flakes in the vicinity of the sanctuary suggest the site region was inhabited long before the Spanish arrived.

Borhegyi's work also led to some startling geological conclusions:

According to Indian legends, the site of the present Sanctuario in Chimayo was originally an Indian shrine....Chimayo is believed to have been a place where fire, smoke, and hot water belched forth in ancient times. The pit of the sacred earth was a pool and was called by the Indians *Tsimajopokwi [pokwi,* "pool," *po,* "water"]. However, according to Tewa legend, when the twin war gods killed ...[a]...giant, fire burst out at many places and the healing, hot mud springs atop Black Mesa, at Tsimmayo [Chimayo], and Obuhegi dried up and only mud was left. The Indians continued to visit the site of the hot spring and used the mud for healing, calling it *nam po'ware [nam,* "earth," *po'ware,* "blessed"].[13]

The area in and around Chimayo was at one time geologically active. As was discussed earlier in the Rio Grande Rift description, there were a good number of explosive volcanoes in the region close to a million years ago. In fact, the Jemez Mountains are actually the severely eroded crater of one of the largest volcanoes on earth. The explosion one million years ago covered the Rio Grande area with billions of tons of ash that has since solidified into the pinkish tan stone so popular with the early cliff dwellers of the region. Up until the 1940s, most geologists did not even recognize that the Jemez Mountains were part of a collapsed caldera. Intriguingly, the Tewa legends predate this time of Anglo confusion.

Since the 1940s, it has been assumed that northern New Mexico was geologically active before people arrived in the area. Perhaps not. Legends and myths always have a germ of truth somewhere within them. The fact that an old Tewa legend mentions "fire, smoke, and hot water belching forth in ancient times" can only mean that someone was around to witness this classic volcanic action. Fire and smoke suggests lava and other pyroclastic materials; hot water and mud suggests geysers. Pueblo Indians, according to Borhegyi's oral history collection, stated that "...the fire burst out from the earth at San Ildefonso, Nambe, and Cabezon." All of these places are in the vicinity of Chimayo.

As to *why* the moist earth supposedly heals, there are two possible explanations: the placebo effect, or there's something in the mud.

The placebo effect has long been known to science. In fact, one scholar in the 1960s concluded that until recently the entire history of medication has been largely a history of placebo effects—that is, benefits obtained from treatments that have value only to the extent that people *believe* they heal.

A placebo is defined as any therapy that heals an ailment without applying any specific treatment to the condition in question: In other words, a sugar pill. People believe a certain thing is medicine and can cure them, and it does! Recently it has been suggested that a placebo, by activating belief, stimulates the body's immune system in some way, thereby causing self-healing. This would explain the relief of some *symptomatic* ailments like minor headaches, superficial skin rashes, or low-level topical infections. But it does nothing to explain the major *structural* changes of the

Student researcher Anne Drabkin sits in the room leading to the Sacred Earth chamber that is filled with anecdotal evidence of healing.

healings recorded at Chimayo: The complete repair of the central spinal column; gnarled, twisted bones becoming straight and healthy within days of a mud treatment; the astonishing reconstruction of knee ligaments within twenty-four hours; and so on.

The second possible explanation for the reputed power of the Chimayo earth is that something is in the mud. Is it possible that through the effects of volcanism, some chemical isotope or blend of elements in some way interact to promote cellular growth in tissue? This would be an easy thing to test in the laboratory. A thorough analysis of the mud by gas chromatography and other evaluations may reveal some intriguing combinations of mineral properties. If something unusual is found in the earth, then it would only be a matter of designing an experiment, complete with damaged tissue samples, to observe changes. Sadly, the last time science looked into Chimayo's dirt was back in the 1940s—the Stone Age with respect to modern laboratory equipment and technique.

Of course, there is a third possibility for the healing effects of

Chimayo earth: Perhaps the ancient Tewa Indians happened upon a special place of great spirituality. Perhaps the ground really is sacred in ways that are not measurable with all the scientific hardware of the twentieth century. Now *that* would be a true mystery!

Contact Persons and Organizations

The definitive article concerning the sanctuary can be found in Stephen Borhegyi's account, "The Miraculous Shrines of Our Lord of Esquipulas in Guatemala and Chimayo, New Mexico," *El Palacio* 63, no. 3, (March 1953).

Another wonderfully descriptive account can be found in Elizabeth Kay's *Chimayo Valley Traditions* (Sante Fe, N.M.: Ancient City Press, 1987).

PUYE CLIFF RUINS
Española, New Mexico

Site Synopsis

High atop an orange-hued mesa one hour's drive south of Taos are the ancient Puye dwellings. Over the centuries, high winds have patiently eroded away the very essence of the adobe structures, leaving only a faint impression of their former earth-colored permanence. Partially excavated in 1907 by Edgar Lee Hewett of the Southwest Society of the Archeological Institute of America, a formal report was never published. In 1909, archeologist Sylvanus G. Morley continued the search for artifacts at the site.

The site was home to over fourteen hundred people who lived there around A.D. 1100. On the side of the high mesa is a carved cave. Above the keyhole opening is a smaller hole, once thought to be an opening for smoke to escape from. During certain times of the year a beam of light enters this hole, casting a daggerlike swath of sunlight across the cave's rear wall. The sunlight illuminates a series of pecked holes during key moments of the year.

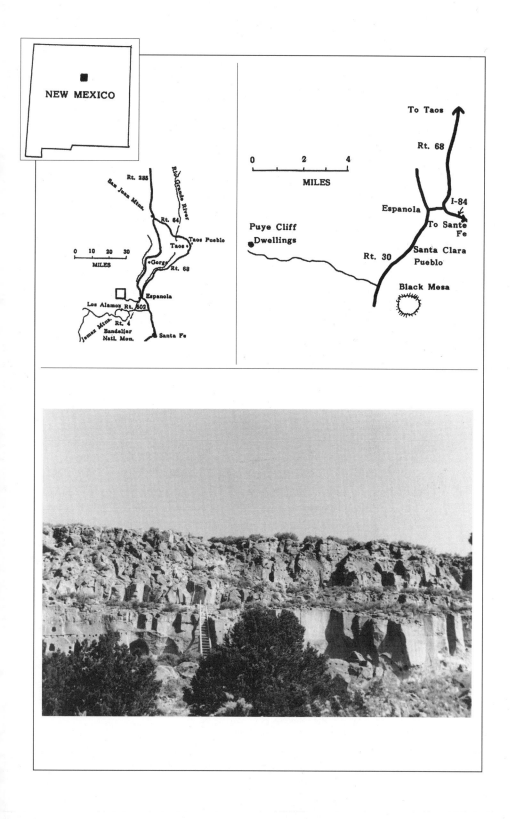

NEW MEXICO

San Juan Mtns.

Rt. 285

Rio Grande River

Rt. 64

Taos Pueblo

Taos

Gorge

Rt. 68

10 20 30

MILES

Espanola

Los Alamos Rt. 502

Jemez Mtns.

Rt. 4

Bandelier Natl. Mon.

Santa Fe

0   2   4

MILES

To Taos

Rt. 68

Espanola

I-84

To Sante Fe

Puye Cliff Dwellings

Rt. 30

Santa Clara Pueblo

Black Mesa

Location

From Sante Fe, take I-285 north toward Española. At Route 502, turn west toward Los Alamos. At the next intersection, turn north on Route 30. Travel for approximately eight miles before turning west toward the well-marked Santa Clara Pueblo Reservation Puye Indian Ruins. Travel for seven miles before turning into the ruin site.

Considerations

The Puye ruins are run and managed by the Santa Clara Pueblo just outside of Española. Observe all tribal customs, which include leaving all artifacts—potsherds, arrowheads, bones, stones—in place. Stopping along the Reservation road leading to the cliff site is prohibited. An admission fee is charged to enter the site.

History/Background

According to tribal elders, the Puye Mesa is the ancestral home of the Santa Clara Pueblo Indians (see Figure 3.7). They have managed the site since 1907. Although this is so, Edgar Hewett made an interesting observation in the 1930s, when he was compiling thirty years of research on the site: "It should not be said that the ancient people of the Pajarito [the region encompassing the Puye Ruins] were the sole ancestors of the communities now living around the margin of the plateau. That there was relationship is no longer questioned, but the degree is yet to be determined."[14] He goes on to say that "evidence on which the hypothesis of identity was based was, mainly, the testimony of the Pueblo Indians themselves."[15]

In the late 1800s, the Pueblo of Santa Clara filed a court case again the United States government for over ninety thousand acres of land lying west of their grant near Española and extending to the Jemez Mountains:

The basis of the claim was an alleged Spanish grant, and in support of such documentary proof as could be adduced, their

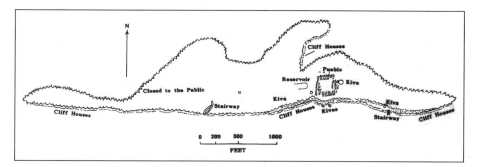

Fig. 3.7. Map of the Puye Mesa (after Hewett, Pajarita Plateau and its Ancient People, author's collection)

homes scattered over the plateau, particularly the Puye village, were pointed out.

This tradition was believed in good faith by the majority of the community. It was a stock argument in pointing out the injustice of the court in granting them a strip of less than five hundred acres along Santa Clara Creek in lieu of the large tract claimed.[16]

In 1907, Hewett held a meeting with the Santa Clara Pueblo elders to discuss excavation of the Puye ruins. During the talks, Hewett came upon some startling information:

They do not contend that their people, in their present organization as a village group, were the original builders of the cliff dwellings and community houses of Puye. They hold consistently to the tradition of a reoccupation of the cliff houses and of some rooms in the great community home by the Santa Clara people during the troubled times of the Spanish occupation.[17]

When asked why elders of the Santa Clara Pueblo don't develop the ruins into a popular tourist attraction like the Taos Pueblo or Bandelier National Monument, the elders at the site tell a chilling and true story.

For years, the ruins *were* a popular attraction. During major festivals, hundreds of people would come, pay admission, and witness

Fig. 3.8. Sunlight streams into this cave, forming a sun dagger. Student researcher Colin Kronewitter points to holes pecked into the rear wall of the cave.

the sacred dances and ceremonies of the Pueblo Indians. One afternoon, after the last white tourist had left for the day, a dark storm cloud appeared out of a clear blue sky. Lightning suddenly burst out of the cloud, killing the two Indian women clad in ceremonial dress who were in a field high atop the mesa. Just as quickly, the cloud drifted away and dissipated. The elders took this as a sign not to popularize the site. Since that day in the late 1970s, the ruins have not been actively publicized, and non-Indians are not invited to attend festivals there.

A previously unknown feature of the Puye site is the presence of a "calendar" cave. Just below the mesa top along the first row of cave dwellings is a dark cave with an oval slit cut above the keyhole entranceway. Sunlight streams through the hole, creating a bright daggerlike image on the dirt floor (see Figure 3.8). Orientation readings suggest that at specific times of the year sunlight flows through the oval, lighting up a pattern of tiny pecked holes at the rear of the cave. Each morning, the sunlight dagger illuminates another peck until the light reaches its extreme position and swings back to repeat the journey.

Although impressive, in the larger context of Anasazi culture, this remarkable awareness of the heavens was rather commonplace. At almost every known Anasazi site in the Southwest, there is structural evidence of either sun- or moon-watching.

Contact Persons and Organizations

Santa Clara Pueblo
P.O. Box 580
Española, N.M. 87532

STONE SPHERES
Los Alamos Canyon, New Mexico

Site Synopsis

In ancient volcanic ash deposits near Los Alamos, New Mexico, are several sites containing stone balls measuring from a few

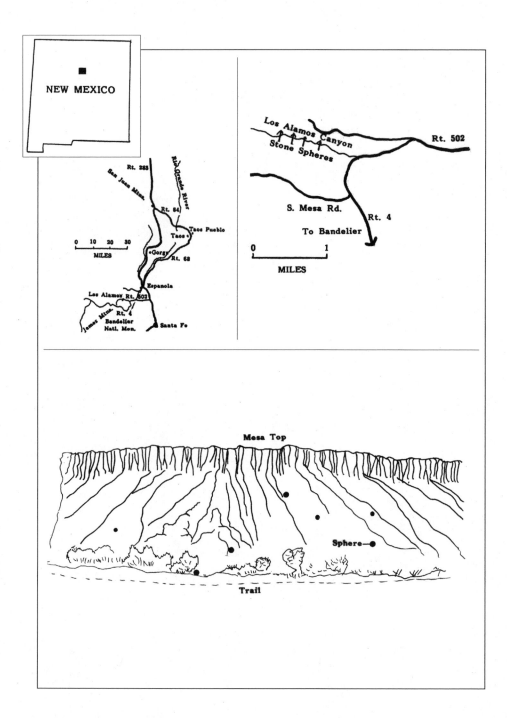

inches to up to two feet in diameter. The spheres are probably the result of the crystallization of volcanic ash in an ancient side vent of the Jemez volcano.

Location

From Sante Fe, take I-285 north toward Española. At Route 502, turn west toward Los Alamos. Stay on Route 502, bearing to the left; the road changes to Route 4. After climbing a hill, the road will fork—follow signs toward Bandelier National Monument. Do not travel on toward Los Alamos. Just before the hill starts to slope upward, about half a mile before the intersection of South Mesa Road (there's a stoplight here), a small parking area will come into view. Park here, climb over the fence, and follow the dirt trail. The mesa top will be on your left. Within a mile you will notice dark spheres within the matrix of the bluff. Look carefully—most are tiny!

Considerations

Los Alamos Canyon is on federal property. Although all citizens have the right to walk on this protected, fenced-in land, all artifacts—geological and human—must remain in place.

History/Background

At the start of World War II, the United States government purchased most of the land in the canyon and set up a secret atomic physics facility there. The mission was to design and build the world's first atomic bomb. The mission succeeded.

The Los Alamos Canyon was formed over one million years ago, when the Jemez volcano exploded and covered the terrain with ash and debris. Erosion carved deep gorges into the soft solidified ash (see Figure 3.9). As the hot ash and gasses flooded valleys and rifts, the molten material closer to the outside air temperature solidified around nucleic particles. As the outer layer of ash cooled, spherical balls were thus produced. Continued ash flow covered over these geological anomalies. Erosion over hundreds of

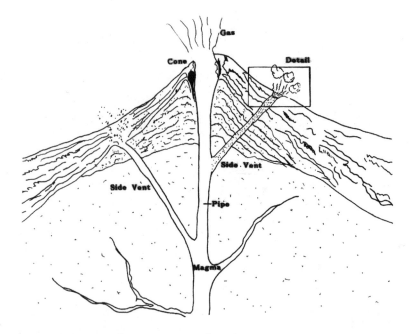

Fig. 3.9. A form of volcano anatomy that suggests a possible origin for the Los Alamos Canyon spheres.

thousands of years exposed sections of the ash matrix in the Los Alamos Canyon, revealing tiny globular spheres (see Figure 3.10).

The Los Alamos Canyon spheres are tiny compared to those found farther south in Mexico. In the late 1960s, Dr. Matthew W. Stirling, writing for the National Geographic Society, reported finding hundreds of gigantic stone balls in an arroyo in southwestern Mexico. The spheres ranged in size from four to eleven feet in diameter. Work by geologists for the Society revealed that they also were the result of volcanic ash crystallizing in constantly growing spheres.

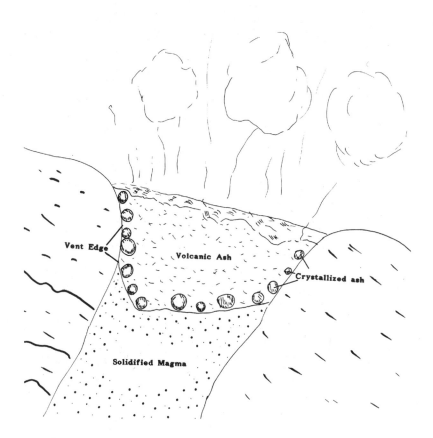

Fig. 3.10. Crystallized ash along vent edge cools into spheres. The erosion of the surrounding soft rock exposes the spheres.

Contact Persons and Organizations

Los Alamos National Laboratory
P.O. Box 1663
Los Alamos, N.M. 87545
(505) 667-5061

TSANKAWI RUINS
Los Alamos Canyon, New Mexico

Site Synopsis

Ten miles due south of Puye are the Tsankawi Ruins of Los Alamos Canyon. Owned by the Department of the Interior and part of the larger Bandelier National Monument, the site has never been fully excavated or surveyed. Little is known about the cultural debris left at the mesa or the cliffside dwellings.

On the cliffs below the mesa top are scores of caves and petroglyphs. Preliminary orientation readings suggest a causal placement of petroglyph styles. The rock art seems to have a pattern of location with respect to key astronomical events like the solstices.

Another mysterious feature at the site is the deeply carved "pathways." Some researchers have suggested that years of ancient foot traffic carved these channels in the soft limestone. A visit to the site will give another impression. It is difficult to believe that anyone would walk through these channels on a regular basis when there are other, safer, nearby rockways to walk over. Perhaps water erosion is responsible. The true purpose of these channels eludes us.

Location

From Sante Fe, take I-285 north toward Española. At Route 502, turn west toward Los Alamos. Stay on Route 502, bearing to the left; the road changes to Route 4. After climbing the hill, the road will fork—follow signs toward Bandelier National Monument. Do not travel on toward Los Alamos. The hill starts to slope upward, and there is a traffic light at the intersection of South Mesa Road. The site is on your left and identified by a large brown sign. Park in the small dirt area and walk in. Stop by the Ranger Station for a trail guide.

Considerations

Tsankawi is part of the Bandelier National Monument, which

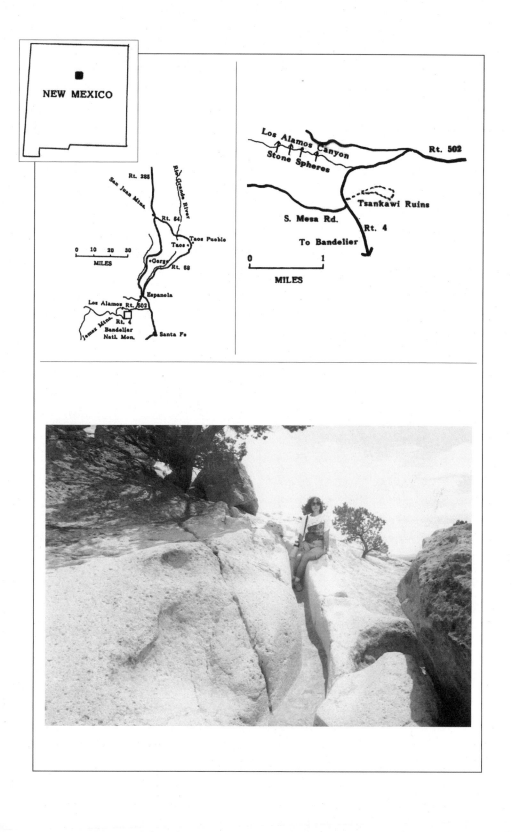

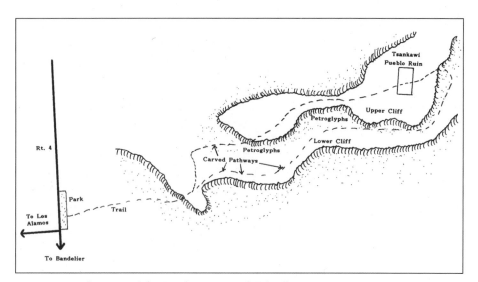

Fig. 3.11. A plan view of the Tsankawi Ruins cliff dwellings.

is part of the National Park Service. Therefore, removal of any objects from this federally protected site is a crime. Leave all artifacts
in place! Future archeologists may need the context of a broken
pot shard or stone to fully understand this mysterious place.

There is a 1 1/2-mile trail that involves some climbing and ne-
gotiating narrow places between rocks. You will need to climb a
rather steep twelve-foot ladder to fully explore the site. Rubber-
soled shoes are necessary. Be prepared for frequent electrical
storms. If you are caught in one, seek shelter in the lower caves.

Tsankawi is only a small part of Bandelier National Monument. The Visitor Center at Monument Headquarters, twelve
miles to the south, contains a rather good interpretive museum regarding the ancient people who populated this area.

History/Background

Bandelier National Monument, New Mexico, was established
in 1916 and encompasses 32,737 acres. Tsankawi is a detached,
unexcavated mesa top twelve miles north of the main Bandelier
site. (See Figure 3.11.)

Fig. 3.12. Researcher Leslie Trento squeezes through one section of the mysteriously carved "trail" at Tsankawi.

Fig. 3.13. A view of a carved "trail" at Tsankawi. The groove here is close to two feet deep.

The many mesas in this area, Tsankawi included, were inhabited by thousands of people from about A.D. 1100 to the late 1500s. Known as the Anasazi, which is Navajo for "The Ancient Ones," these people probably migrated from the Chaco Canyon region when the conditions there worsened. Known as the Rio Grande Anasazi, these people were all interdependent. The people at Tsankawi, for example, were not isolated from other villages located on nearby mesas and in canyons. There was probably trade in tools, pottery, corn, beans, blankets, and jewelry among the many pueblos. In fact, many of these neighboring towns probably competed for various resources like firewood and game.

Researchers estimate that the large ruined pueblo at Tsankawi had over 350 rooms, and in some areas it was over three stories

Fig. 3.14. Assorted petroglyphs at Tsankawi. The meaning of these strange symbols is not known to modern researchers.

high. Hand-and-foot cut steps in the cliffside below the pueblo connect it to the carved caves.

One of the oddest features of this site are the carved so-called foot trails (see Figures 3.12 and 3.13). While a number of sites in the area have footpaths that have been worn down by generations of Anasazi feet, sections of the Tsankawi trail are close to three

Fig. 3.15. Student researcher Jennifer Person stands beneath an elaborate panel of rock carvings.

feet deep and only one foot wide. It is hard to imagine anyone ac-tually using these awkward "trails" for movement throughout the village without having to twist and contort the body. In fact, near the deepest cuts there is evidence of alternative paths that were worn down. We're left with the question, What were the deep grooves used for? And why are they in specific sections of the cliff top? The entire mesa is composed of the same volcanic ash, which

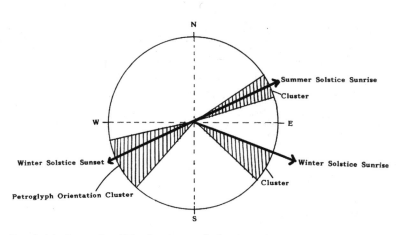

Fig. 3.16. A sample of Tsankawi petroglyph orientations.

presumably erodes at a constant rate throughout the site, so it is unlikely that natural erosion wore down these trail sections. They were consciously carved deep into the stratum. Why?

The placement of petroglyphs at the Tsankawi site bears discussion. Scattered throughout the upper and lower cliff walls are scores of pecked and incised images from another age (see Figures 3.14 and 3.15). Hundreds of these symbols and designs grace the flat cliffsides. But a close inspection reveals that only certain sections of the cliff walls were used for this purpose. Many times a host of petroglyphs graces one flat-walled section while another protruding section of rock face—right next to it—is untouched. Why? Is there a pattern? Over the past few years, teams of my students have taken simple orientation readings detailing which way the rock markings face. Their sample data is intriguing. Certain types of images seem to favor certain directions. Human-type symbols seemed to face in a southwesterly direction, and the spiral designs seem to be pecked to face a different direction. Furthermore, when we plotted out the general orientation of our sample of one hundred petroglyphs, we found that they show a decided favor for the key solar orientations: the winter solstice on December 21, and the summer solstice on June 21. A person looking at many of these petroglyphs on those dates would see them lit by the rising and setting sun! (See Figure 3.16.)

Contact Persons and Organizations

Bandelier National Monument
HCR 1, Box 1, Suite 15
Los Alamos, N.M. 87544-9701
(505) 672-3861

OTOWI RUINS
Los Alamos Canyon, New Mexico

Site Synopsis

On the highest point on a mesa top within sight of the
Tsankawi Ruins is a large pueblo ruin. Clusters of cliff dwellings
abound in this little-visited site. Pottery fragments are scattered
throughout the slopes.

Location

From Sante Fe, take I-285 north toward Española. At Route
502, turn west toward Los Alamos. Stay on Route 502, bearing to
the left; the road changes to Route 4. After climbing the hill, the
road will fork—follow signs toward Bandelier National Monument.
Do not travel on toward Los Alamos. The hill starts to slope upward, and there is a traffic light at the intersection of South Mesa
Road. Turn right at the intersection (west). Travel for one mile before pulling off the right shoulder onto a small, dirt parking area.

Although the mesa top is fenced in, it is accessible to all citizens. Carefully lift up the barbed wire fence to get in. Follow the
dry streambed toward the mesa. Climb up the talus slope toward
the top. Several partially excavated caves and thousands of pottery
shards can be seen here.

Considerations

This site is federally protected; leave all material found within
the fenced-in area in place.

NEW MEXICO

Rt. 285

Rio Grande River

San Juan Mtns.

Rt. 64

Taos Pueblo

Taos

Gorge

Rt. 68

0 10 20 30

MILES

Espanola

Los Alamos Rt. 502

Rt. 4

Jemez Mtns.

Bandelier
Natl. Mon.

Santa Fe

Los Alamos Canyon

Stone Spheres

Rt. 502

Otowi Ruins

Tsankawi Ruins

S. Mesa Rd.

Rt. 4

To Bandelier

0   1

MILES

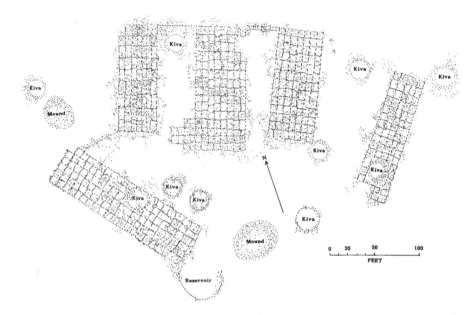

Fig. 3.17. Ground plan of Otowi Pueblo Site (after Hewett, Pajarita Plateau).

Do not walk too far west. Although a large chain-link fence separates the Los Alamos National Laboratory land from this site, there is a government shooting range right next to it. Stray bullets have been known to hit the talus slope. Stay clear of this western edge.

History/Background

Otowi is intriguing because few people visit it, and even fewer know of its existence. Most tourists to northern New Mexico zoom past en route to the Los Alamos Visitor Center or to the highly publicized Bandelier National Monument, some fifteen miles to the south.

While climbing about the slopes and mesa top at this site it is easy to project oneself back in time. Very little has changed save the climate and brush growth. This is a peaceful place that commands striking views of the land. When it was well watered it must have been an Eden.

Otowi was partially excavated by Edgar Hewett in 1905 under the auspices of the Smithsonian Institution. Hewett concentrated mainly on the numerous burials found in caves and mounds. Close to twenty percent of the skeletal remains were infants. Ceremonial food bowls, polishing stones, and awls were found in abundance. Intriguingly, very few projectile points—arrowheads, axes, and other implements used in war—were found at the site. In fact, the entire nature of the mesa and dwellings suggest a people at great peace with their surroundings.

Several large earthen mounds were looked into by Hewett's group. Ten kivas remain visible (see Figure 3.17).

As one walks around Otowi, the voices of the thousands of people who lived, laughed, and loved atop this gorgeous mesa can almost be heard.

Contact Persons and Organizations

Edgar L. Hewett's description of this intriguing site, although terse, remains the best: *Pajarito Plateau and its Ancient People* (Albuquerque: University of New Mexico Press, 1938).

Los Alamos National Laboratory
P.O. Box 1663
Los Alamos, N.M. 87545
(505) 667-5061

Southwestern New Mexico

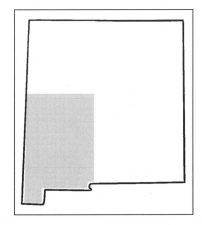

Geologically, southwestern New Mexico differs from the north-central region. While the northern part of the state is torn by a continental rift and millennia of volcanic action, southwestern New Mexico is an eroded former sea bottom that resulted in mountain blocks of sand and limestone. Tall cliffs of resistant 200-million-year-old sandstone tower over valleys and gullies filled with shale, mudstone, and fine silt.

SANDSTONE PIPES
Laguna, New Mexico

Site Synopsis

Many hundreds of cylindrical sandstone columns—termed *sandstone pipes*—are exposed in the Laguna, New Mexico, area. They cut nearly horizontal strata some 180 million years old.

Location

From Sante Fe, travel south on I-25 toward Albuquerque. At Albuquerque, exit west on I-40. Travel for thirty-five miles, exiting at the 117 Mesita interchange. At the exit ramp end, turn left (northwest) onto the small road that parallels the interstate. Do not go into Mesita. Within three miles, several mesas and sandstone columns (on both sides of the road) will be visible.

Considerations

Do be careful when you park on the side of the road. The pipes are on private property, so bring along a powerful pair of binoculars to scan the terrain from the road.

History/Background

The pipes in this region range from a few feet to a few hundred feet high and a few inches to one hundred fifty feet wide. Each pipe is composed of sandstone.

The pipes originated during the sedimentation of the uppermost bluff they were contained in. They probably formed in part when sand sank into compacted mud and erosion brought the collapse of the underlying gypsum, over 180 million years ago (see Figure 3.18).

The site is intriguing because it forces one to consider geological time. One of the more difficult concepts in geology is to recognize and truly understand the vast amounts of time that certain features represent. The time of our own lifespan compared to

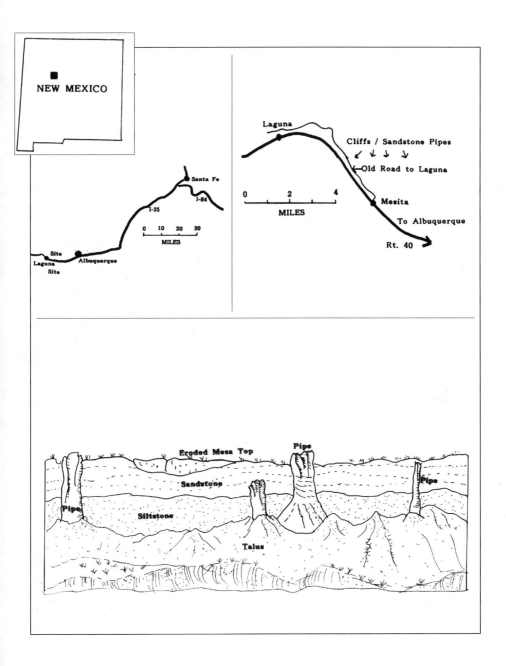

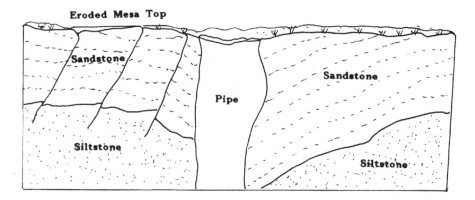

Fig. 3.18. Detail of pipe and rock strata (after Schlee).

that of the age of the earth, for example, makes for some very difficult comparisons: 75 years versus 3.9 billion years. The Laguna sandstone pipes had their start when dinosaurs roamed the planet!

Contact Persons and Organizations

An excellent article on these weird formations is John S. Schlee's "Sandstone Pipes of the Laguna Area, New Mexico." *Journal of Sedimentary Petrology* 33, no. 1 (March 1963): 112–23.

INSCRIBED PEBBLES
Buckhorn, New Mexico

Site Synopsis

Hundreds of small stones found along an old streambed have unusual etchings and carvings on them. Cross-sectioning of these stones suggests they were naturally formed.

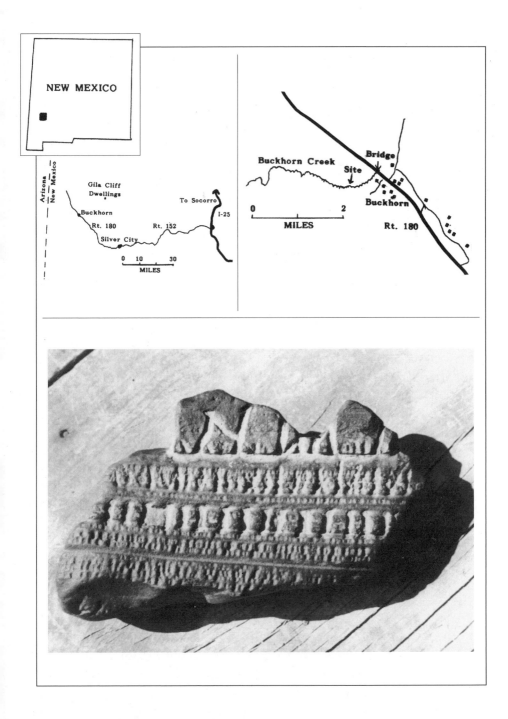

Location

From Sante Fe, travel south on I-25 for 225 miles. Turn west at Route 152 near Caballo. Continue on Route 152 for sixty miles, whereby you will reach Silver City. At Silver City, take Route 180 northwest for thirty-five miles, stopping at Buckhorn. Cross over the one intermittent stream and park well off the side of the road. Walk west along the streambed for about half a mile, looking closely for small pebbles with surface grooves.

Considerations

As with most land in the West, this area is usually owned by someone—either the federal government, a rancher, or a ranching company. Take care to observe any posted signs and barbed wire fences as you look for etched rocks over this vast area. Don't limit yourself to this one stream. There are several sites along the road-side.

History/Background

Researcher Bill McGlone is responsible for publicizing these unusual stones. In the mid-1980s, ranchers living in the area brought these stones to the attention of epigraphers (people who study ancient script). Some of these individuals actually claimed to translate the markings in a variety of ancient Old World lan-guages. McGlone looked into the matter, and through a collabo-ration with geologist George Morehouse, who sliced open the stones along the suspected "writing," concluded that the markings were caused by erosion. Rock thin-sectioning revealed that the grooves extended well into the rock as natural fissures (see Figure 3.19).

The astonishing thing about these stones is how similar they are to inscriptions. There's a regularity to the markings that fooled even the best geologists prior to the cross-sectioning. The mystery, of course, is, How did they get that way? And why do they only ex-ist over a small area near a stream in southwestern New Mexico?

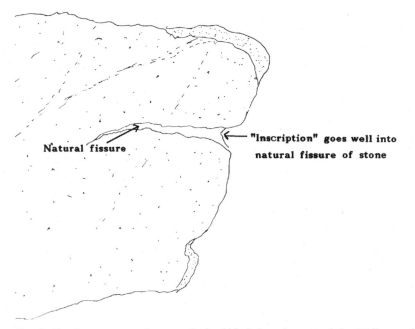

Natural fissure

← "Inscription" goes well into
natural fissure of stone

Fig. 3.19. Cross section of an inscribed pebble (after photograph by William R. McGlone).

What is unique about the geology of this area? Some suspect that ancient volcanism is responsible in a way not yet understood. Perhaps the unusual matrix of stones comes from a vent or dike that still needs to be identified. Even then, we are left with the mysteriously beautiful symmetry of the natural inscriptions.

Contact Persons and Organizations

An excellent place to examine McGlone's work is his recently published book, *Ancient Inscriptions: Plow Marks or History?* (Sutton, Mass.: Early Sites Research Society, 1994).

Background information on the geology of the region can be obtained from the nearby Gila Cliff Dwellings National Monument: Route 11, Box 100, Silver City, N.M. 88061; (505) 388-8201.

CITY OF ROCKS STATE PARK
Southeast Grant County, New Mexico

Site Synopsis

Along the southwestern corridor of New Mexico are several eroded masses of rock that jut out of the ground like buildings in a city.

Location

Travel south on I-25 from Albuquerque to Las Cruces, a distance of some 315 miles. At Las Cruces, travel west on I-70 for fifty-one miles to Deming. At Deming, exit on Route 180 going toward Silver City. After about twenty miles, turn northeast on Route 61, traveling for about three and one-half miles before the turnoff for City of Rocks State Park. Watch for signs.

Considerations

As with all state parks, care must be exercised not to ruin the site. That means no climbing on rocks or taking any artifacts.

History/Background

"Rock cities" exist in many parts of the West. In fact, later in this book there's a site listed in Idaho that shares many superficial similarities with the one listed here.

Sixty million years ago, southwestern New Mexico was inundated with explosive volcanoes. Both slow-oozing shield and violent cinder-cone volcanoes spread their geological havoc over the region. There was major ash deposition in this area. Over millions of years the volcanic ash and cinders compacted to form rock known as *tuff*. Volcanic tuff is prone to the differential erosive effects of wind and rain. This means that the stone weathers in odd conical shapes. This has yielded a cluster of stone structures that, from a distance, look like city buildings, or castles, or sentries, or just about anything else a daydreaming or sun-stricken mind can conjure up.

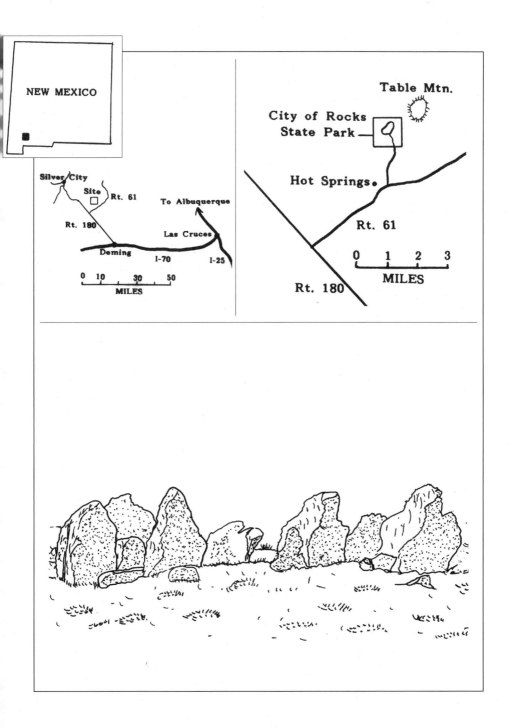

Sixty million years ago saw the development of the first mammals. Occasionally the odd fossil can be found in the matrix of solidified ash making up these stone masses.

The best time to see this site is during a summer sunset, when the shadows are long, the light is golden red, and the air gets cooler. Although the geology of the site is well known, the stone clusters seem strangely ominous. Perhaps the beckoning night causes our imagination to evoke the odd, the unusual. This is not a peaceful place.

Contact Persons and Organizations

One of the best books from which to get an overview of the general geology of New Mexico is Halka Chronic's *Roadside Geology of New Mexico* (Missoula, Mont.: Mountain Press Publishing Company, 1991). Even though it only touches upon the City of Rocks site, it does provide superb background information for understanding the region's complicated geology.

PATTERNED GROUND MOUNDS
Animas Valley, New Mexico

Site Synopsis

Scattered throughout the Animas Valley in New Mexico are hundreds of polygon-shaped mounds measuring eighty to ninety feet in diameter. The origin of this "patterned ground" is uncertain. Various hypotheses indicate differential weathering.

Location

Travel south on I-25 from Albuquerque to Las Cruces, a distance of some 315 miles. At Las Cruces, travel west on Route 10 for 115 miles to Lordsburg. Continue on Route 10 for ten more miles, turning south on Route 338. Travel on Route 338 toward Animas, a distance of about twenty-five miles. Continue past Animas. In six miles you will pass the rodeo arena on your left. After

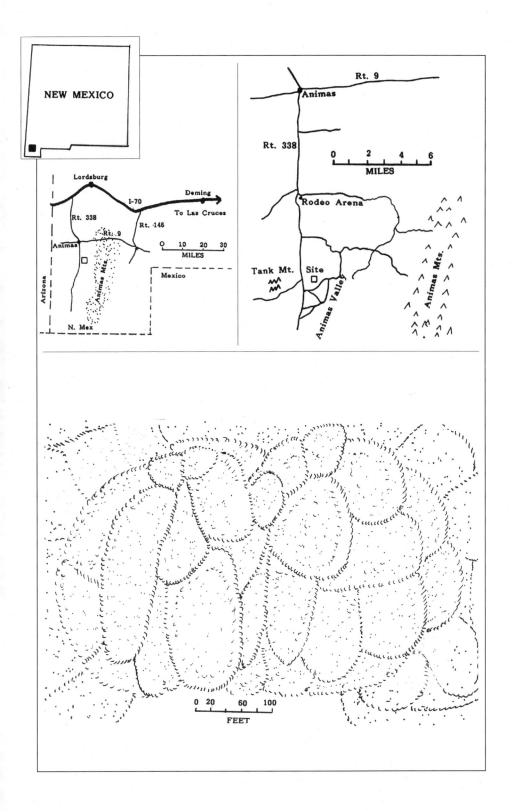

another six miles, turn east onto the adjoining road. Within two miles you will see the ground patterns off the road to the north.

Considerations

The ground patterns are on private lands, so look but please do not walk out onto the land.

These patterns are very difficult to detect. The best time to see them is after a *light* dusting of snow, or during the rainy late-spring season.

History/Backgorund

There are many places throughout the Rocky Mountain West where peculiar ground formations exist. In the Washington State chapter of this book, for example, is another example of odd moundlike patterns.

In the early 1950s, many researchers focused on these strange bits of geological puzzles. Maxwell Knechtel, working for the U.S. Geological Survey, warned his colleagues in 1951 that superficial resemblance of ground patterns in areas of ancient glacial conditions to those of nonglacial conditions can be confusing. By 1956, A. L. Washburn reviewed the scientific literature on the subject and came up with a grand classification scheme to describe the weird polygon shapes that nature occasionally dishes up.

The strange-looking polygonal patterns found in the Animas Valley are enormous, some ranging from eighty to ninety feet in diameter. They are very difficult to detect from the ground. The physical marks upon the surface are broad, faint depressions averaging about three feet wide and one inch in depth. Their straight, trenchlike appearance gives them away. Two species of plant tend to grow along the cracks of these massive polygonal forms, thereby making them quite obvious from the air.

The Animas Valley forms are probably the result of the ground drying up on a regular basis over long periods of geological time. The effects of wind and heat apparently cracked the earth in this region into strange and massive shapes. But just why this happened in one section of the Animas Valley and not elsewhere is unknown.

Contact Persons and Organizations

A good article on strange ground formations by Walter B. Lang is "Gigantic Drying Cracks in Animas Valley, New Mexico." *Science* 98, no. 2557 (December 31, 1943): 583–84.

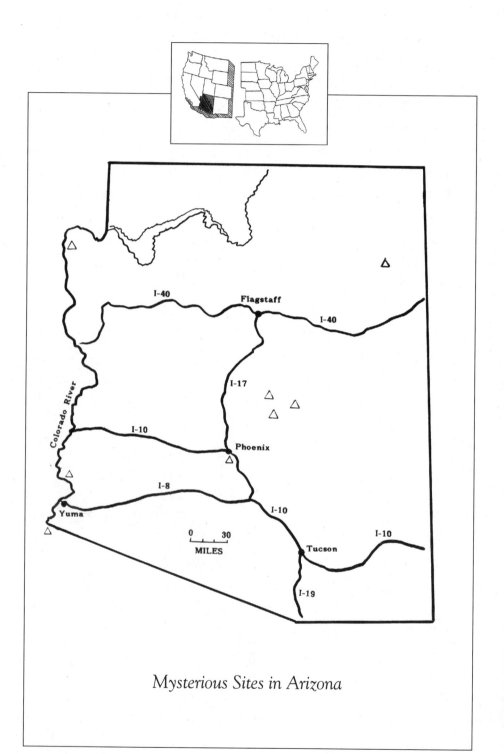

Mysterious Sites in Arizona

4

Arizona

Arizona is a state of mountains, high mesas, and forests. Stretching across the state from the northwest to the southeast is a region known as the Mexican Highlands. To the southwest of this band of mountains is the great Sonoran Desert.

Although first explored by Spanish conquistadors in the early sixteenth century, the land remained remote and relatively unpopulated by Anglos due to its rather hot and arid climate. But with the damming of many rivers, the Colorado first among them, large artificial reservoir lakes were created. With stored water came the great population shift to this region of recent decades.

North-Central Arizona

The north-central region of Arizona encompasses one of the most astonishing cuts within the earth's crust: the Grand Canyon. First partially explored by the early Spanish, the canyon was *terra incognita* for hundreds of years. By the mid-1800s, however, the United States Congress, with the cajoling of the Department of War, thought it important to find out exactly *what* was in the canyon and whether the Colorado River was navigable. Several expeditions attempted to find

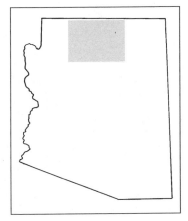

out. One was successful in surveying this bizarre place. Its early sense of awe and mystery is recorded here.

1857–1858 IVES EXPEDITION UP THE COLORADO RIVER
Arizona

Site Synopsis

The first American to experience and write about the mystery of the Colorado River's deep inner canyons was Lieutenant Joseph C. Ives of the Corps of Topographical Engineers. In 1857 Ives was assigned the task of determining whether the Colorado River was navigable. If it was, it would be of immense value for transporting supplies to various military posts in New Mexico and Utah.

Ives and crew did the impossible. They had a "mini" steamboat built in Philadelphia, had it transported in pieces by ship to the Isthmus of Panama, where it was taken by train to the Pacific Coast, put back on a ship, and then transported to San Francisco. It was then sailed by schooner around the Baja Peninsula, up through the Sea of Cortez to the Gulf of California, and onto the mouth of the Colorado River, where it was reassembled for the journey. For the next six months Ives and his men steamed upriver over three hundred miles before setting out on mule to explore vast stretches of the Grand Canyon. Although only seventy-five miles of the river was navigable, Ives wandered into portions of the Colorado that had never been seen by white men before. He also mapped part of the Grand Canyon for the first time. The trip was one of daring and courage.

Location

The Ives Expedition started where the Colorado River meets the sea, in the upper Gulf of California. The city of Yuma in modern Arizona, but then a military outpost, was a stopping point on this remarkable journey. Today, the heavy use of the river for the

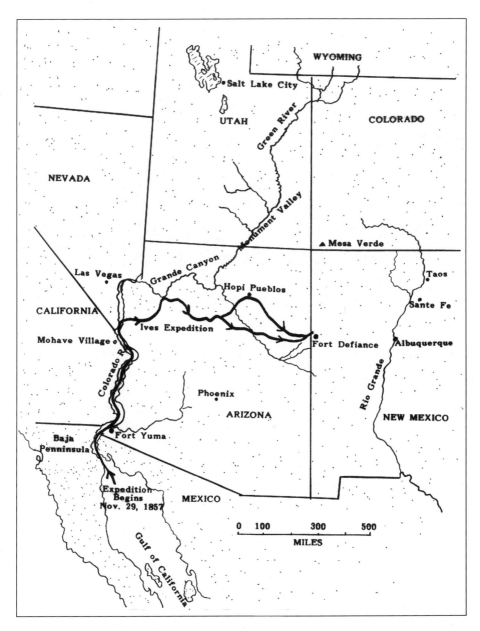

The route of the 1857–1858 Ives Expedition up the Colorado River.

An engraving of the steamboat Explorer, *used by Lieutenant Ives to explore three hundred miles of the Colorado River. (Reprinted from Ives,* Report upon the Colorado River of the West, *author's collection)*

water needs of the American Southwest has virtually dried the flow to a mere trickle. Furthermore, the six dams on the Colorado stretching from Denver to the Mexican border have made the once-mighty river into a placid stream. It would be impossible to duplicate Ives's water journey today. One can, however, hike into various parts of the Grand Canyon to get some idea of the gorgeous terrain he encountered.

Considerations

Much of the land from Yuma north to Bullhead City is on an Indian reservation. Please abide by all tribal regulations, which usually include a stipulation that visitors cannot leave their cars and wander around the land unless special permission is granted.

History/Background

In 1857, John B. Floyd, the secretary of war, commissioned Lieutenant Ives to find out how far the Colorado River was navigable. In the mid-1800s, very little was known about the Colorado River. While the northern and southern sections were familiar, the midsection—the area we now know as the Grand Canyon—was completely unknown. Nonetheless, some portions of the river were among the earliest parts of America to be explored.

Fifty years after Columbus landed on Watlings Island in the Bahamas, Spanish missionaries were trekking up the Colorado. In fact, Ives reported in his account of his expedition that more information about the river was obtained in the early 1500s than in the three subsequent centuries.

In 1540, Francisco Vasquez de Coronado traveled through the territory now called New Mexico. A detachment of his men led by a Señor Dias traveled westward. They discovered the Colorado, naming it—*Colo,* "Red" and *Rado,* "River"—and following it south to its mouth.

Another of Coronado's captains, named Cardinas, reached far into the river's course. Cardinas's account of the trip states that "after twenty days' march, over a desert, they arrived at a river, the banks of which were so high that they seemed to be three or four leagues in the air."[1] Some of the men tried to climb down to the river but gave up after reaching impassable areas. This was the first description of the Grand Canyon. After this time most people simply avoided the great impasse of the canyon, opting to cross New Mexico and the Arizona region well south of the canyon.

Ives started his journey in late November. At the mouth of the Mojave Canyon (near the present Lake Havasu City) he experiences the wonder and mystery of place:

> An abrupt turn at the base of the apparent barrier revealed a cavern-like approach to the profound chasm beyond. A scene of such imposing grandeur as that which now presented itself I have never before witnessed. On either side majestic cliffs hundreds of feet in height, rose perpendicularly from the water. As the river wound through the narrow enclosure every turn developed some sublime effect or startling novelty in the view. Brilliant tints of purple, green, brown, red, and white illuminated the stupendous surfaces and relieved their somber monotony. Far above, clear and distinct upon the narrow strip of sky, turrets,

An engraving of Ives and crew steaming through the Mojave Canyon of the Colorado River.
(Reprinted from Ives, *Report*)

spires, jagged statue-like peaks and grotesque pinnacles over-
looked the deep abyss.[2]

It's remarkable to read Ives's description. He is acutely aware of
and very able to describe all that surrounded him, from the stillness of a pinkish red canyon to the physical features of the Yuma
Indians. Later in his report he writes:

The waning day found us still threading the windings of this
wonderful defile and the approach of twilight enhanced the wild
romance of the scenery. The bright colors faded and blended
into a uniform dark gray. The rocks assumed dim and exagger-
ated shapes and seemed to flit like giant specters in pursuit and
retreat along the shadowy vista. A solemn stillness reigned in
the darkening avenue, broken only by the splash of paddles or
the cry of a solitary heron, startled by our approach from his
perch on the brink of some overhanging cliff.[3]

Anyone who has traveled through a canyon at twilight knows exactly what Ives experienced. The feeling remains the same today as it was 140 years ago.

As the crew continued into unknown territory, Ives makes a rather interesting cultural observation about the Mojave Indians that he has come into contact with:

> In most respects they think us their inferiors. I had a large crowd about me one day and exhibited several things that I supposed would interest them, among others a mariner's compass. They soon learned its use and thought we must be very stupid to be obliged to have recourse to artificial aid in order to find our way. [4]

How intriguing. It's taken over a century for many Americans to reject technology as the world's savior. Here we have an "un-contaminated" indigenous population so in tune with their environment that such an "artificial aid" as a compass is considered dumb. Are some of us today even more dependent upon artificial aids?

Later in the journey, as they steamed into the entrance to the Grand Canyon, Ives notes that, as far as any records go, they are approaching a locality that had never been visited by whites:

> We...entered its gigantic precincts and commenced to thread the mazes of a canyon far exceeding in vastness any that had been yet traversed. The walls were perpendicular and more than double the height of those in the Mojave mountains, rising, in many places, sheer from the water, for over a thousand feet....The river was narrow and devious and each turn disclosed new combinations of colossal and fantastic forms, dimly seen in the dizzy heights overhead, or through the sunless depths of the vista beyond. With every mile the view became more picturesque and imposing, exhibiting the same romantic effects and varied transformations that were displayed in the Mojave Canyon, but on an enlarged and grander scale.

About where Lake Mead is today, Ives determined not to continue, because the river was filled with ascending rapids and a very swift current. He continued on by mule. But before doing so he left

A view of the Grand Canyon as recorded by the Powell Expedition. (Reprinted from Powell, *Exploration of the Colorado River West and Its Tributaries*, author's collection)

Side canyons of the Flax River near the Grand Canyon, as recorded by Ives's team. The canyon made a powerful impression upon all who ventured into it then, as it still does today. (Reprinted from Ives, Report)

one of the most sublime descriptions of an unexplored area yet encountered. Lieutenant Ives was astonished and moved by the grandness of all he saw:

> The canyon continued increasing in size and magnificence.... Wherever the river makes a turn the entire panorama changes and one startling novelty after another appears and disappears with bewildering rapidity. Stately facades, august cathedrals, amphitheaters, rotundas, castellated walls, and rows of time-stained ruins, surmounted by every form of tower, minaret, dome, and spire, have been molded from the cyclopean masses of rock that form the mighty defile. The solitude, the stillness, the subdued light, and the vastness of every surrounding object, produce an impression of awe that ultimately becomes almost painful.[6]

Ives wrote on the spot. At the end of a day he religiously recorded his impressions in his journal. The true, almost photographic quality of his musings come forth loud and clear. His voice

The Grand Canyon as recorded by the Powell Expedition, showing amphi-theaters and sculpted buttes. (Reprinted from Powell, *Exploration*)

continues to speak to us today of the mystery of a trip up the Colorado River into the Grand Canyon.

In 1869, Major John Wesley Powell, a Civil War veteran who had lost his right arm in battle, rafted down the Colorado with a party of nine men. Starting on the northern route, from Green River City, Wyoming, Powell directed a survey into the very bowels of the canyon. His efforts led to a detailed map of this last unknown area of the West. The steel plate engravings gracing his report to the Smithsonian lend an air of mystery and intrigue that still permeates the region today.

Contact Persons and Organizations

The best place to get acquainted with the Ives Expedition is to get hold of the Ives report (see the Bibliography for the specific citation). Large metropolitan and university libraries should have it, or be able to get it.

The Grand Canyon looking west from To-ro'-weap. (Reprinted from Powell, Exploration)

Grand Canyon National Park
P.O. Box 129
Grand Canyon, AZ 86023
(602) 638-2401, -7888

Central Arizona

Central Arizona is a vast valley desert studded with saguaro cactus and, today, man-made scenery. With the completion of Roosevelt Dam in 1911, the once wild Salt River was tamed and the desert took on that peculiar look typical of artificial irrigation: It bloomed with farms and towns. Central Arizona was the most populous part of the region before white settlement. It still is today, thanks to modern irrigation.

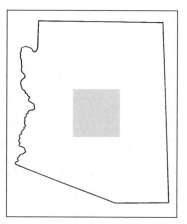

PREHISTORIC IRRIGATION CANALS
Salt River and Gila River valleys, Phoenix, Arizona

Site Synopsis

The Salt River and Gila River valleys are intersected by a vast network of ancient canals. The city of Phoenix in the late 1800s followed the lines of one of these canals. The extent of the canals can be appreciated when the size of the Salt River Valley is considered: over 250,000 acres. The original canals with their laterals must have exceeded one thousand miles in length.

The canals are now attributed to the ancient Hohokam Indians. Some can still be traced today in the Arizona desert.

Location

While most of the irrigation canals of this remarkable ancient people lie underneath the roads and buildings of modern Phoenix,

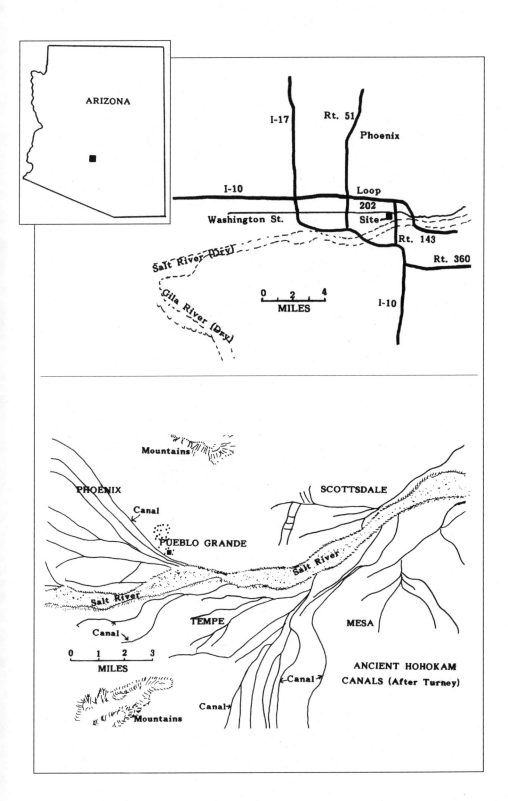

ARIZONA

I-17   Rt. 51   Phoenix

I-10   Loop
Washington St.   202
Site
Rt. 143
Rt. 360

Salt River (Dry)

Gila River (Dry)

0   2   4
MILES

I-10

Mountains

PHOENIX   SCOTTSDALE

Canal

PUEBLO GRANDE

Salt River

Salt River

TEMPE   MESA

Canal

0   1   2   3
MILES

Canal

ANCIENT HOHOKAM
CANALS (After Turney)

Canal

Mountains

the Pueblo Grande Ruins and Museum, located on Washington and 44th Street in east Phoenix, offers a firsthand look at the structures.

From Phoenix, take Arizona 202 east, exiting south at the intersection of Arizona 143. Travel south. The site is on Washington Street.

Considerations

Pueblo Grande is a registered National Historic Landmark; observe all signs and warnings.

History/Background

Almost two thousand years ago, the Hohokam (a Pima expression meaning either "old ones" or, rather endearingly, "all used up") settled along the Salt River Valley a little way from modern Phoenix. Over the next few hundred years the Hohokam people built a large village now called Pueblo Grande. This community included homes, storage rooms, activity areas, several ball courts, cemeteries, and a platform mound. Pueblo Grande existed because the Hohokam constructed several hundred miles of irrigation canals that fed their fields. The labor involved in this activity was astonishing. In fact, it is suspected that the canal system supported a community of over twenty thousand people.

Sometime about A.D. 1450, about 150 years before the Spanish explored the area, like many sites in the Southwest, Pueblo Grande was mysteriously abandoned. Silt from rainstorm washouts filled in most of the canals, while the constant erosive action of water slowly turned the adobe homes and mound into piles of mud. There are many theories about why the Hohokam left: disease, warfare, and, most intriguingly, increased salt deposits from overirrigation.

In 1929, Pueblo Grande Park was created to preserve, interpret, and house Hohokam artifacts. A series of excavations extending up to the present were mounted to unravel the mystery of these industrious people.

Today, as one walks through the museum and partially excavated platform mound, it is easy to understand the attraction of the surrounding land: remove the modern artifacts of cars, houses, and an airport, and the valley is gorgeous. The land is also very fertile, given vast amounts of water. Two thousand years ago the Ho-hokam, who initially built pit houses dug into the ground, developed above-ground adobe architecture and a knack for diverting water over 250 miles. Their foresight was the precursor of the water-delivery system used today for the city of Phoenix. If their mysterious disappearance actually was due to the salt deposits collecting in their canals, then we need to learn from their mistakes. Perhaps building a modern city in the desert that's dependent on water being transported over many miles is a recipe for disaster. It happened to the Hohokam. It can happen to modern Phoenix.

Contact Persons and Organizations

The best place to get information on this Hohokam site is the Pueblo Grande Ruins and Museum, 4619 East Washington Street, Phoenix, AZ 85034; (602) 495-0901. Fax: (602) 495-5645. The museum is open from 9:00 A.M to 4:45 P.M. Monday through Saturday, and from 1:00 P.M. to 4:45 P.M. on Sunday. There is a small admission fee.

An excellent book about the site can be purchased at the museum or from the museum through the mail (twenty-five dollars plus three dollars shipping and handling): *Archaeology of the Pueblo Grande Platform Mound and Surrounding Features*, edited by Christian E. Downum.

GIGANTIC ANCIENT CIRCULAR RINGS
Tonto National Forest Area, Arizona

Site Synopsis

Faint circular patterns are scattered over the central portion of Arizona. These circles are nearly perfect in outline. They range in size from four to over one hundred miles in diameter. Geologists suspect they are the fracture-descendant impressions of a 4-billion-year-old meteor attack.

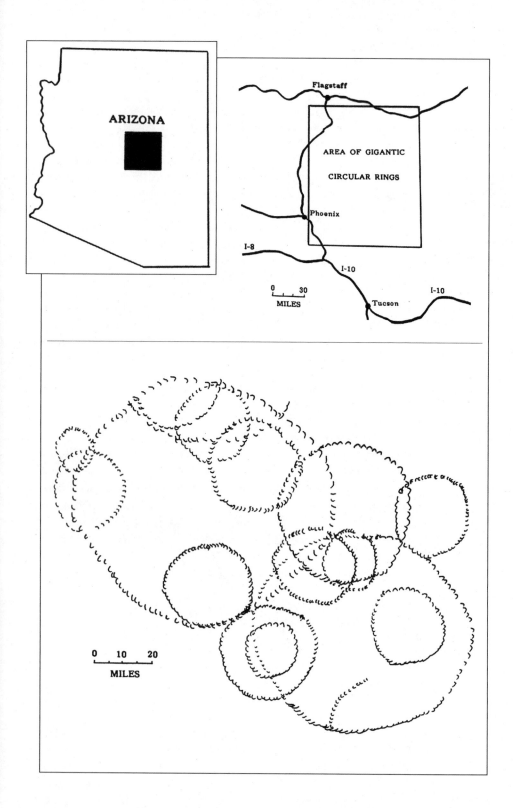

Location

Generally north and east of Phoenix.

Considerations

This site breaks from the pattern of this book of describing sites that can be visited. It is impossible to see the circular impressions from the ground—they are too big. One must either fly overhead or, better, study topographic raised-relief maps to see the patterns. They are bizarre and overwhelming.

History/Background

In the late 1970s, researcher John M. Saul analyzed several raised-image maps of Arizona. To his astonishment, he saw large circular impressions. He theorized that these ring formations had something to do with mineral deposits and found that they were indeed related: minerals like copper, lead, gold, zinc, and silver were always associated with a ring formation.

At the time, geologists speculated that the circles were the remnants of meteor impacts when the earth's primordial crust was just solidifying, some four billion years ago. Apparently the meteorites were so damaging to the crust that they fractured it well below the surface. As the crust solidified, it maintained the scar of impact.

One of the more intriguing observations made by Saul is that "The positions of many towns, roads, railroads, rivers, lakes, and reservoirs seem to be related to circles...."[7] Perhaps this is due to the topography caused by the circle—the mountains, ridges, and such. If so, then it is interesting to realize that the location of so many people in Arizona is the product of some vastly ancient cosmic event.

Contact Persons and Organizations

John Saul's original article is the best introduction to these bizarre formations: "Circular Structures of Large Scale and Great

Age on the Earth's Surface," *Nature* 271 (January 26, 1978): 345–49.

Tonto National Monument
P.O. Box 707
Roosevelt, AZ 85545
(602) 467-2241

Northeastern Arizona

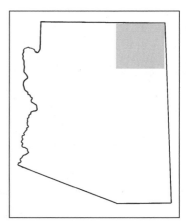

Northeastern Arizona is a land of monuments, canyons, and intrigue. While seemingly one of the most inhospitable places in the world, it is surprising to see evidence of ancient ruins scattered throughout this entire region. In the late 1800s a concerted effort was made to explore and map out this strange countryside.

1874–1876 HOLMES AND JACKSON EXPEDITIONS
Southwest Colorado/Northwest New Mexico/Northeast Arizona

Site Synopsis

In 1874, geologist William H. Holmes and noted western photographer William H. Jackson separately explored the ancient ruins of the Southwest. Several elaborate, well-illustrated government reports were compiled.

At the time of exploration, the boundaries of the southwestern territory were not strictly defined. There is some overlap between states in this section.

Fig. 4.1. Noted western photographer William H. Jackson sketched this cliff dwelling in the Canyon de Chelly, northeastern Arizona, in 1874. (Reprinted from Hayden, Tenth Annual Report)

History/Background

Under the guidance of field geologist Ferdinand Hayden, Holmes and Jackson made a relatively complete survey of the region. Their teams covered nearly six thousand square miles chiefly in Colorado but also including the adjacent territories of New Mexico, Utah, and Arizona. Unlike Simpson's team, who saw and sketched the ruin sites as a footnote to their primary mission, Holmes and Jackson set out to specifically study and map the sites during the years 1874 through 1876. Their reports are filled with systematic surveys and steel engravings of the ruins. The true wonder of these accounts is to see the walled cliffside dwellings through the eyes of men who were studying them for the first time—before they knew anything about the Anasazi builders (see

Figures 4.1 and 4.2).

These men were venturing into the unknown. Atop every mesa was a ruin with crumbled sand, sage, stone, and thousands of painted pottery shards strewn about. By examining the drawings that accompanied their reports, we may see a world that existed for centuries untouched by maps, rangers, and tourists (see Figures 4.3 and 4.4).

Some of these sites are inaccessible today due to Reservation or Park Service mandate.

Contact Persons and Organizations

One of the most knowledgeable persons on the early expeditions to the Southwest is George Robinson, owner of G. Robinson's Old Prints and Maps in Taos, New Mexico. Mr. Robinson is an expert on the minutiae of these and other ex-

Fig. 4.2. Two miles down from Canyon de Chelly, photographer William H. Jackson discovered a cliff house some two stories high. (Reprinted from Hayden, Tenth Annual Report)

peditions. He also has an impressive collection of maps and prints from these jaunts for sale. His store is located at 124-D Bent Street, Taos, N.M. 87571; (505) 758-2278. Fax: (505) 758-1606.

The Western History Collection of the Denver Public Library is one of the best sources for these reports, as is the University of Colorado at Boulder, which was and still is a repository for government publications.

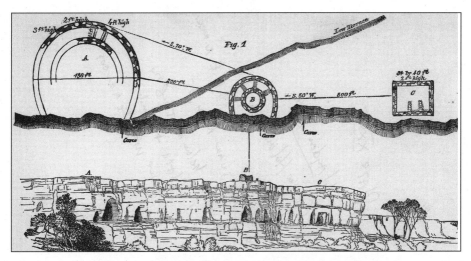

Fig. 4.3. In 1875, explorer William H. Holmes discovered and sketched a series of cliff dwellings on the San Juan River in northwestern New Mexico some thirty-five miles below the mouth of the La Plata River and some ten miles above the Mancos. (Reprinted from Hayden, *Tenth Annual Report*)

An engraving of Casa del Eco, twelve miles below Montezuma Creek in the southwestern Colorado–southeastern Utah region. William H. Jackson discovered this massive circular cave some two hundred feet in diameter and one hundred feet deep. (Reprinted from Hayden, *Tenth Annual Report*)

Fig. 4.4. William Holmes sketched a reconstructed image of the tower found above the mesa in the cliffside ruins along the San Juan River in northwestern New Mexico. (Reprinted from Hayden, Tenth Annual Report*)*

Between Montezuma and Hovenweep Creeks in southwestern Colorado—southeastern Utah, William H. Jackson found small cliff houses on the tops of many mesas. (Reprinted from Hayden, Tenth Annual Report)

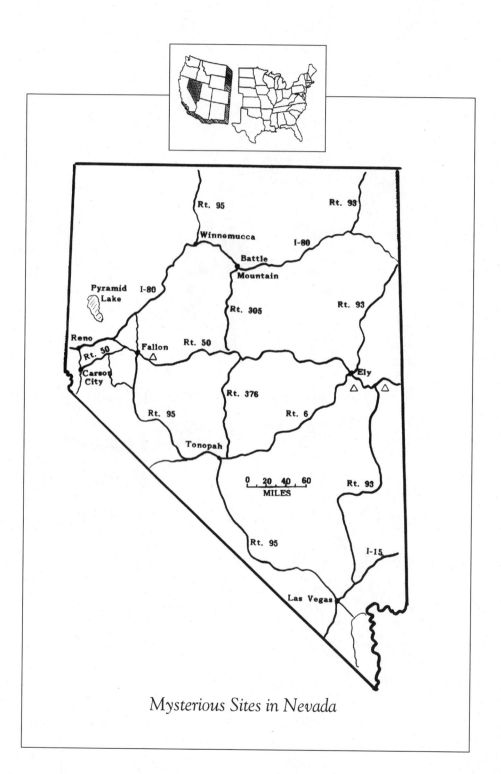

Mysterious Sites in Nevada

5

Nevada

Nevada lies east of the high Sierra Nevada. It owes its extraordinarily dry climate to this mountain range, which blocks the movement of moist clouds inland.

Nevada was one of the last areas in the continental United States to be explored. It wasn't until the early to mid-1800s that scientific expeditions ventured seriously into this region.

West-Central Nevada

After Las Vegas in the southeast, the west-central region of Nevada contains most of the state's population. The remainder of the state is sparsely populated; one can drive for miles and see no people. The terrain evokes a different feel under such conditions.

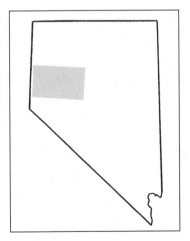

ACOUSTIC SAND MOUNTAIN
East of Fallon, Nevada

Site Synopsis

In the eastern part of Churchill County, Nevada, about twenty-five miles east of Fallon there is a hill of sand about four miles long and a mile wide. The whole dune ranges from one hundred to four hundred feet high. When someone walks upon this dune, or when the sand slides, it emits a sound resembling the vibrating of a telephone wire. The sound can be so intense that it is sometimes heard up to seven miles away. Various people have described the sound as ranging from that of a short note on a bass viol to a roaring boom.

Location

Take Route 50 east from Fallon for twenty-five miles. Watch for the sign to Sand Mountain.

Considerations

There are several loose-sand spots in this region: Watch for the warning signs.

History/Background

For as long as people have walked across desert sand they have heard sounds. The history of musical sands is extensive and intriguing. Stories from the Middle East speak of sand sounding like the harps of angels. Along the western Sinai Peninsula near the north port of Tor, natives lyrically describe the acoustic sand there to be from a buried monastery's wooden gong.

In other parts of the world sand "booms like thunder, crunches like snow, barks like a dog or squeaks like a mouse." One gets the impression that the recorders of such sounds might have been out in the sun too long. That's actually not the case. The acoustical

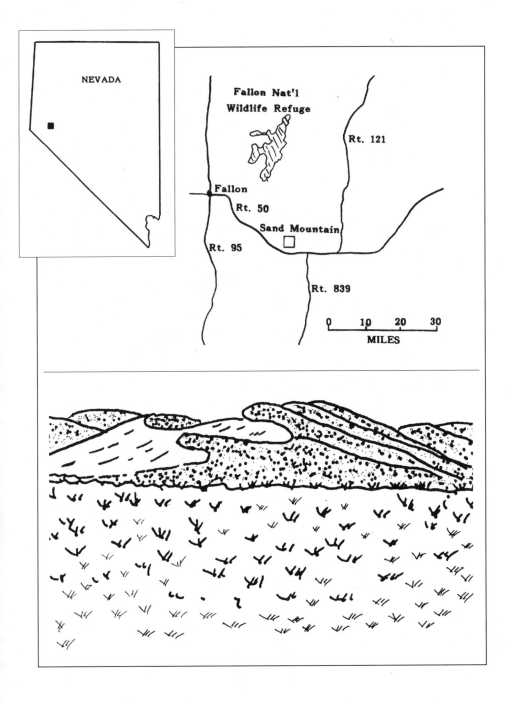

properties of sonorous sand have been carefully studied and described in several scientific articles.

Sand Mountain, east of Fallon, Nevada, was first described in
an 1883 article. It was described as being one hundred to four hundred feet in height and about a mile wide and four miles long. The
grain particles were said to be extremely fine. The sliding sand,
caused by the wind or a running animal "...makes a noise resembling the vibration of telegraph wires with a hard wind blowing,
but so much louder that it is often heard at a distance of six or
seven miles, and it is deafening to a person standing within a short
distance of the sliding sand."[1]

The definitive study on sound-producing sands was produced
by geologist John F. Lindsay in 1976. In an extensive investigation
of sand from around the world, Lindsay and a team of scientists
showed that the sound comes from the size and shape of the sand
particles slipping and sliding over one another. In fact, the scientists discovered that two distinct types of sound are produced:
"booming" sand and "squeaking" sand. Each sound is the result of
the grain's size and composition. Furthermore, squeaking sand is
"...dependent upon the sand being well sorted, well rounded, and
highly spherical."[2] Booming sand, on the other hand, depends on
very dry sand and on grains that are not well rounded but
nonetheless highly polished.

The scientists conclude with the following observations:

- Booming sand produces sound in the narrow-frequency
  range of 50 to 180 hertz.
- Sand Mountain in Nevada fits into the booming category.
- Booming sand is uneven, highly polished, and very dry.
- Squeaking sand produces sounds in the range of 500 to 2,500
  hertz.
- Squeaking beach sand consists of very large quartz grains
  that are highly spherical.

So we know all there is to know about acoustical sand, right?
Wrong. We still don't fully understand how the great variety of
sounds are made. Furthermore, why are musical sandy beaches specific to area—why are they so localized, even on the same beach?

To truly understand the bizarre nature of this site, you need to walk over the dunes and hear the sounds emanating from your feet. It's an unnerving experience that will quickly bring up mystical feelings, even with all the scientific explanations of sound-producing sand.

Contact Persons and Organizations

The best description on the science of musical sand can be found in John F. Lindsay's article "Sound-Producing Dune and Beach Sands." *Geological Society of America Bulletin* 87 (1976): 463–73.

East-Central Nevada

East-central Nevada was actively explored by Lieutenant George M. Wheeler in the late 1860s. During his mapping expeditions he noticed many unusual features, among them a massive cave in the eastern part of the state.

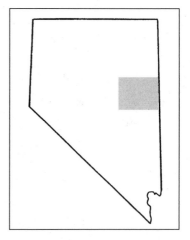

CAVE VALLEY CAVE
Cave Valley, north of Conner's Pass, Humboldt National Forest, Nevada

Site Synopsis

First described by the Mormons in 1858, the Cave Valley Cave has been the focal point of many weird legends. During his astonishingly comprehensive surveys of the Nevada-Utah region, Lieutenant George M. Wheeler's party made the first known sketch of the site.

Location

From Ely, take Route 93 south for ten miles until you reach Route 486. At this junction take Route 486 (Steptoe Creek Road)

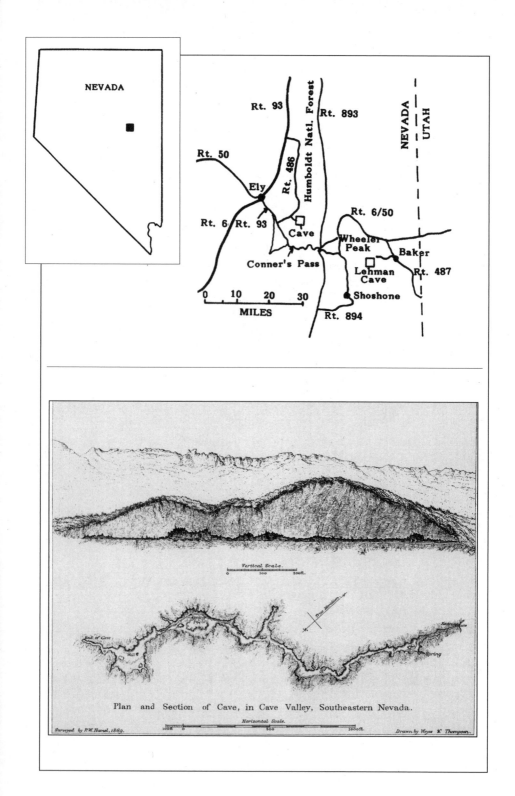

Plan and Section of Cave, in Cave Valley, Southeastern Nevada.

Vertical Scale.

True Meridian.

End of Cave.   *Wall.*   *Spring.*

Horizontal Scale.

Surveyed by P.W. Hamel, 1869.   *Drawn by Weyss & Thompson.*

north five miles before turning east onto a small campground road—look for signs to Cave Creek Reservoir. Take this road for a little over a mile. Pull off to the side of the road and look at this magnificent hidden cave!

Considerations

There are no guides, lights, or Disneylike attractions at this cave. It is dangerous. A brief glance at the engraving done by Wheeler's party over one hundred years ago attests to this.

If you plan to find this cave, contact the National Park Service at Great Basin first. Let them know what you're up to.

Reread the Fulford Cave Considerations, on page 000, for information on caving equipment, safety, and other details.

History/Background

On March 20, 1858, George Washington Bean, a twenty-six-year-old Indian interpreter, explorer, and guide, set out from Provo, Utah, under the orders of Mormon leader Brigham Young. The objective of the expedition into the Nevada desert was to find hiding places for Utah Mormons in the event that they were invaded by a hostile United States Army. This explains Bean's interest in a rather large cave found west of the Schell Creek Range in Cave Valley, Nevada. He wrote:

> In the first valley west of the rim is discovered a large cave having numerous smaller branches. The main cave is half a mile in length and varying in breadth from five to sixty feet. The smaller caves or branches are from ten feet to one hundred yards in length and from ten to twenty-five feet high. The first half is perfectly dry, the remainder have a damp clayey bottom. And we found three pools of water, cold but having a mineral taste. *There were thousands of tracks of human beings also the appearance of fires being lighted in many places, through the entire length of the main cave.* There was also the track of a wild animal, supposed to be that of a wolverine. The air in most parts of the cave was

good, but rather warm in some places. The entrance was about four feet high and six feet in breadth. The mountain over the cave is low and of solid rock, probably not more than eighteen to twenty feet from the natural ceiling of the cave. *The Indians in the immediate neighborhood, for generations past (according to their own statements) have not had the hardihood to enter this cave,* but when they saw us go in and stop about an hour and return in safety, we prevailed upon one brave to accompany us on our second exploration. *They have a legend that two squaws went into the cave, a long time ago, and remained six months. They went, in perfect nudity and returned dressed in fine buckskin and reported they had found a large and beautiful valley inside, clothed, with vegetation, timber, water, and filled with game of the choicest species. Also, a band of Indians in an advanced state of civilization, being dressed like white men. They assert the tracks we found were made by these subterranean inhabitants.* I am satisfied they were made by Indians in former times, going into the cave to get clay to make earthenware, as numerous pieces of broken ware are scattered over different portions of the country. It was probably a tribe called Mosquis (or white Indians of the Colorado valley); as we learned they once inhabited this country.[3] [Emphasis added.]

Eleven years later, in 1869, Lieutenant George M. Wheeler led a survey team into this very same valley. During the mapping expedition, his men re-explored and sketched the cave that the Mormon team found (see Figure 5.1). Wheeler wrote that:

Its exploration was made by a party of 23 to a right-line distance of 3000 feet from the orifice, developing walls of 700 to 800 feet in height, with dry chambers from nearly 2,000 feet of the distance, the balance approaching the sink at the furthest distance from the opening, showing the presence and action of percolating waters, reaching a pit apparently terminal for this level which it was found impracticable to explore for lateral connections, that may, for all that is known, extend in any direction.[4]

Caves are strange places. When we look through the Bean and Wheeler descriptions it is clear that something strange was going on at the Cave Valley Cave. For example, why would the Indians

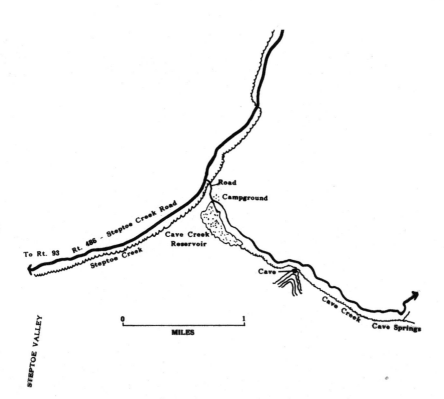

Fig. 5.1. Site map to Cave Valley Cave, Nevada.

interviewed by Bean have a bizarre legend about white men living in the cave? Where did the tracks come from? Could they be from the ancient inhabitants of the valley who roamed into the cave in search of clay, as Bean suggests? And if so, if the clay was so good for pottery, why didn't later generations of Indians use this source? And where did these "cave visitors" go? Why was the cave taboo to the tribes met by Bean? Perhaps the early cave visitors stumbled upon the true power of this site.

Throughout the Americas, underground caverns have always been recognized by the indigenous population as places of great spiritual power. It was almost universally accepted that these places should be used as sites for invocation to the forces of nature. At Chichén Itzá, in the Yucatan, there is such a cavern, where the ancient and modern Mayans attempted to stimulate the spirits to bring rain by leaving offerings far into the recesses of the cave.

Descent into the underworld is a universal theme in cross-cultural mystical experiences. A cavern can be seen as a gateway to the underworld or a passageway for earth spirits. Or, looked at another way, cracks in the earth bring to the surface the influences of the earth goddess. Aside from the obvious elements of darkness and mystery associated with caverns, why do they have such a universal appeal? As indicated at the start of this book, some scientists speculate that fissures in the earth's crust in some way influence the human neurological network. The thinking is that slight changes in the magnetic properties of the earth's crust, as indicated by earth cracks, allows variations in magnetic/gravitational pull. This fluctuation, in ways not fully understood, affects perception. Anecdotally, the Americas, and indeed the world, are filled with stories of people descending into caverns and coming out with a renewed sense of balance, insight, and perception. American Indians would periodically go into caverns and other dark areas to commune with the spirit world, to achieve wisdom through vision quests.

Could the Cave Valley Cave be a site where a generation of ancient people left the region after a collective vision inside the cavern told them to? Were the Indians met by Bean merely reflecting folk memories of this ancient abandonment?

Contact Persons and Organizations

Great Basin National Park
Baker, NV 89311
(702) 234-7331

Lieutenant Wheeler's firsthand account (in Volume 1 of his *Surveys*) is *must* reading before a visit to this cave. See the full citation in the Bibliography.

LEHMAN CAVES
Baker, Great Basin National Park, Nevada

Site Synopsis

In eastern Nevada is a remarkable cave that extends into the side of a mountain for several hundred feet. The cave is filled with a plethora of cave formations, some of which drip from the ceiling, and others of which ooze out of tiny cracks in the limestone. One type of cave feature, known as a *shield*, has several mysterious explanations to account for its formation.

Location

From Ely, take Route 93 south for thirty-one miles before turning north on Route 6/50. Route 6/50 curves around the base of Wheeler Peak. Travel on this road for fifteen miles, turning off toward the town of Baker, which is on Route 487. Follow the signs from Baker to Lehman Caves.

Considerations

This cave is well lighted. Tours are given on a regular basis by Park Service employees. Good rubber-soled walking shoes are advisable for the path throughout the cave.

History/Background

Found and developed as a cave attraction in 1885 by Absalom Lehman, a participant in the 1849 California Gold Rush, the site owes its origin to a vastly different time.

Over 550 million years ago, Nevada was covered with a great inland sea. Over millions of years, tiny shelled marine animals died, leaving portions of their bodies on the sea bottom. In time these calcium remnants solidified into limestone. Some twenty million years ago, when the mountains of Nevada formed and the inland sea evaporated, Lehman Caves had their beginning.

Caves form when rainwater percolates through plant matter

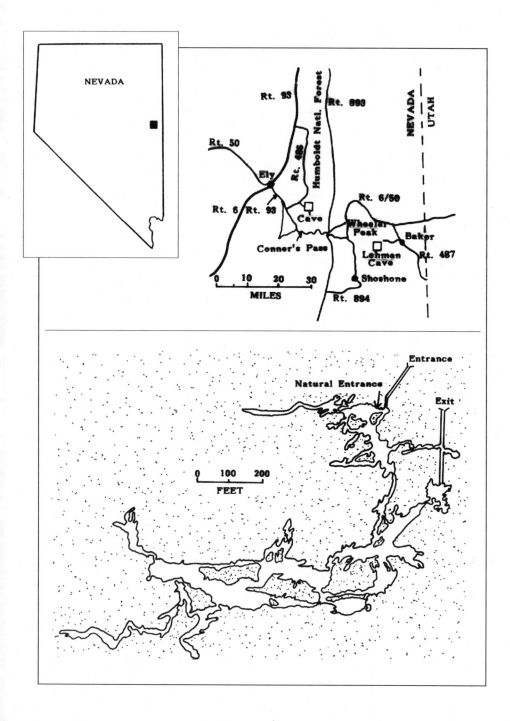

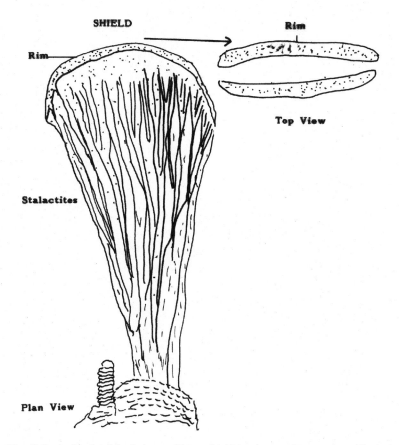

Fig. 5.2. A sketch of the Lehman Caves shield in plan, and a top view. Note the crack between the rim sections.

and limestone, producing a weak form of carbonic acid. Carbonic acid slowly seeps through natural rock cracks, dissolving the limestone. Given enough time, fissures turn into giant caverns. When the carbonic acid reaches the water table of underwater streams, the level of dissolving action increases. In essence, the multitude of rooms at Lehman Caves were hollowed out by underground water, which later drained away.

Stalactites are iciclelike formations that hang from a cave ceiling. They are formed when carbon dioxide–ladened water drips slowly through cave ceiling cracks. If the droplet enters a waterless cavern, the carbon dioxide is released from the drop and the mineral calcite that has been in solution attaches to the cave ceiling. Eventually, one drop at a time, the calcite deposition gets larger, forming what's called a "soda straw." Minerals deposit on this thin tube and slowly build up. Sometimes gravity shapes the formation into a slender projection.

Lehman Caves has hundreds of stalactites and assorted flowstone covering the walls. By far the most intriguing are the "shields." Shields look like rounded clam shells that are split down the center and covered with many flowing stalactites (see Figure 5.2). One theory to account for these strange formations suggests that water pushes out of a rock-wall crack and slowly builds into an elliptical structure. Another theory suggests that the moon's gravity pulls apart the earth's joints and cracks. This motion, it is believed, allows for the slow ebbing of calcite deposits through cracks and fissures. This might also explain why there are no calcite deposits within the two halves of the shield—the motion of the crust breaks any mineral deposition.

Caves are strange places that allow one to enter a world completely alien to sunlight. Lehman Caves is a startling introduction into this bizarre underworld.

Contact Persons and Organizations

Great Basin National Park
Baker, NV 89311
(702) 234-7331

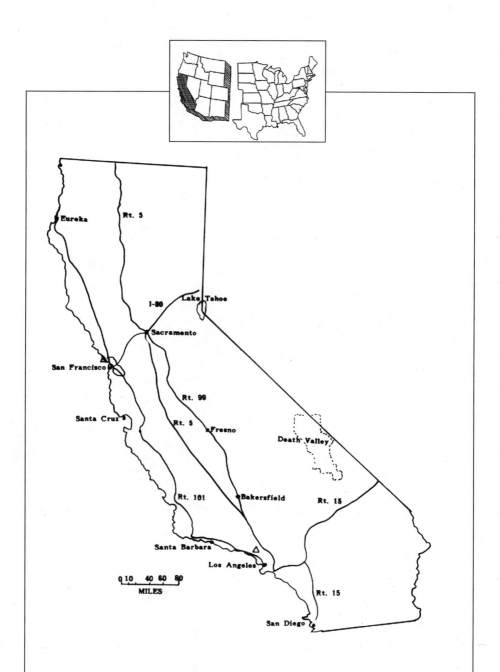

Mysterious Sites in California

6

California

California was named by Spanish explorers for an island paradise in a sixteenth-century novel. It has beckoned travelers and dreamers ever since.

The state is filled with divergent topography: lush redwood forests and sierra mountains to the north, dry desert to the south. Irrigated central valleys have become a cornucopia of cash crops during the last century of watering. The state is cut by a series of major geological faults, the most famous being the San Andreas, which leveled San Francisco in 1906. The fault goes right through the heart of downtown San Francisco. Scientists talk not of *if* there will be another major earthquake, but rather of *when*.

Southwestern California

Southwestern California is a dry, semi-arid land that, incredibly, has become home to millions of people. Lured by the glitz of the movie industry and the lushness of the irrigated central valleys, the area around Los Angeles has become a mecca for small and large business. The congestion of sprawling Los Angeles, a mind-boggling city encompassing some 450 square miles, is curiously offset by the serenity of the surrounding mountains. The Santa Monica Mountains, which run from the Hollywood

221

An engraving of the canyon of Psuc-See-Que Creek, in California. (Reprinted from United States Pacific Railroad Expedition & Surveys—California and Oregon)

Hills to Malibu Beach and beyond, is an area that still is only partially developed. Rugged terrain and a certain wildness still can be felt in these parts. A drive along the Mulholland Highway, a fifty-five-mile parcel of paved and dirt road that stretches from Hollywood to the Pacific Ocean, brings one back to the serenity of presettlement southern California.

WINTER SOLSTICE
SUNRISE PETROGLYPHS
Burro Flats, Simi Hills, Los Angeles, California

Site Synopsis

In a small cave in the hills northwest of Los Angeles are ancient Indian markings. During the midwinter solstice a beam of light illuminates a maze of paintings.

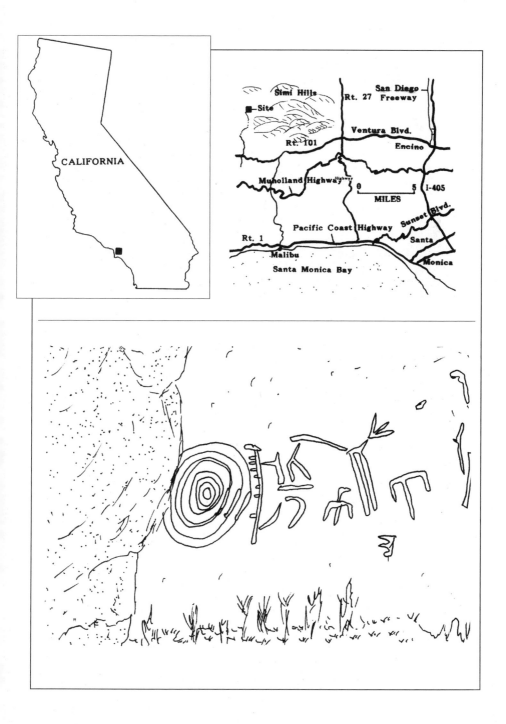

Location

From Los Angeles, take the San Diego Freeway, I-405, north to Ventura Freeway, Route 101. Take this road west for approximately twenty-three miles, passing such towns as Tarzana and Woodland Hills. About three and one-half miles past the intersection of Route 101 and Dry Canyon Road at Calabasas, there's a confusing winding trail—Las Virgenes Canyon Road—leading up to the Simi Hills. Five miles up this road you'll enter Bell Canyon. Take the first left turn—going north—and in two miles you'll reach an intersection. Turn west (left) on this road. Travel for two and one-half miles. At that point you'll see the clearing of Burro Flats: Straight ahead the road snakes between two cliffs. Park in the first clearing before entering the hills. You'll see several rock overhangs and a small crevice opening.

Considerations

Watch for snakes, mountain cats, and human prowlers. Don't light any matches in this dry region!

This is a difficult site to find and get to. I recommend the purchase of the Calabasas, California, 1:50,000 scale topographic map. Topographic maps can be found at most good sporting goods or hunting stores. And see Figure 6.1.

History/Background

Just northwest of the fire-ravaged Santa Monica Mountains in the Simi Hills high above the city of Los Angeles is an area known as Burro Flats. The mysterious Chumash Indians of the region once decorated many of the rocks there with a host of strange, almost hallucinogenic paintings of humanlike figures with wings, handprints, concentric rings, and long creatures with multiple legs.

The Chumash made their home along the high ground of the Pacific Coast from San Luis Obispo to Malibu Canyon. Their villages included several family homes and a ceremonial enclosure.

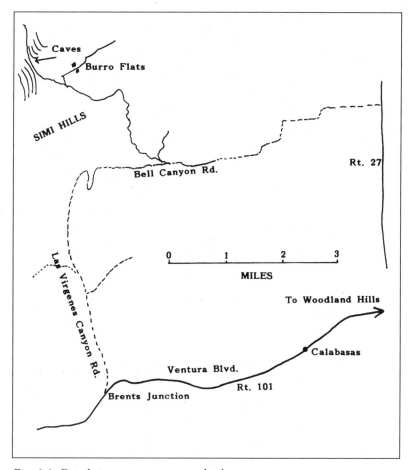

Fig. 6.1. Detail site map to cave petroghyphs.

Shamans were relied upon to bring rain, cure sickness, and guarantee a large food supply.

In one rock shelter in the midst of their ancient homeland, during the winter solstice—December 21—a beam of light passes by the series of entry rocks and strikes one of the concentric ring paintings. The image is striking. Legend has it that long before the Spanish first set foot into this special land, Chumash shamans retired to the cave once a year to watch for the arrival of the light. Soon after this particular splash of sunlight, the days would get longer. The observance of the winter solstice told the shaman that winter was half over. In a sense, this place was a calendar. But it must have been more. When one views the vast array of strange and bizarre paintings within the cave, it is easy to speculate. Some researchers go so far as to suggest that mind-altering drugs were commonly used by shamans to alter their consciousness during the solstice. Perhaps the paintings are drug-induced. Perhaps they are the product of a profound spiritual experience. This place demands attention.

The juxtaposition of the rugged tree-lined hills here with ur-ban, smog-infested Los Angeles to the southeast gives one pause. Only a few miles away are the seeming endless miles of bland paved highway and fast-food chains. Yet here, during late Decem-ber, visions of this land in its days before white settlement may be found.

Contact Persons and Organizations

> Santa Monica Mountains National Recreation Area
> 30401 Agoura Road, Suite 100
> Agoura Hill, CA 91301
> (818) 597-9172, -1036

Northwestern California

As one travels north along Route 1, an inspirational road that hugs the Pacific coastline of California and affords an aston-ishing view of the ocean, the state's geolog-ical framework becomes evident. The fault zones slicing through California have cre-ated, over eons, a ruggedness of landform that defies understanding. Massive hills near Monterey swoop down to the sea, craggy hillsides of red sandstone and granite show their beauty along several roadside rock cuts. Northern California has long been a place of meditation and inspiration.

In the 1960s, several metaphysical institutes and inward-looking training centers set up shop along the Santa Lucia Range. Poets and writers throughout the twentieth century have ventured into this region searching for the muse. Early Spanish explorers looked for gold among the hills. But long before the incursion of European culture into this mysterious land, the indigenous population of California worshipped here.

SACRED CIRCLE
Mount Tamalpais State Park, north of
San Francisco

Site Synopsis

On a hilltop north of San Francisco is a circular formation of rock outcrops that were sacred to the Miwok Indians. Why?

Location

From San Francisco, take Route 101 across the Golden Gate Bridge. Travel for about four miles, passing Marin City, until you see the turnoff for Route 1, just west of the town of Manzanita. Travel west on Route 1 toward the coast. One-half mile from the coast is a winding road (Frank Valley) leading north to Mount Tamalpais State Park. Turn up this road, and within two miles the circular arrangement of stones can be seen. Pull off to the side of the road and experience magic.

Considerations

This spot is a popular jumping-off point for hang gliders, so if the weather is nice and the thermals just right, expect lots of people milling about. Few are aware of the antiquity of this site, so don't be alarmed at the cavalier attitude of most people. Educate them.

History/Background

Just across the Golden Gate Bridge north of San Francisco is the Marin Peninsula, a prong of land that encompasses some of the

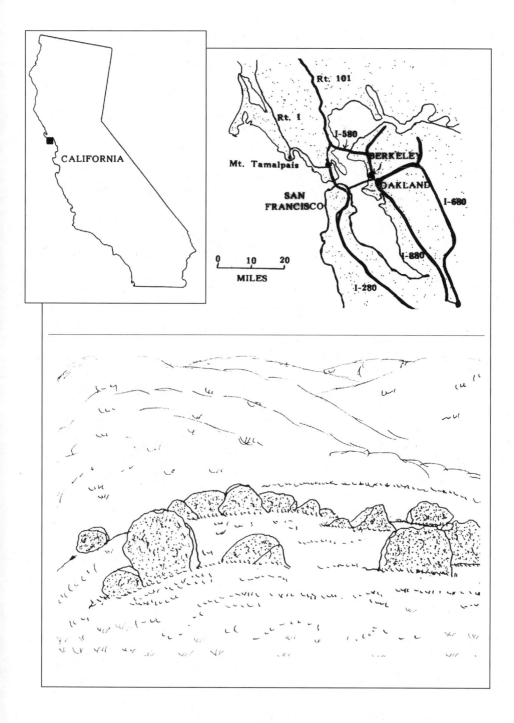

most beautiful landforms in the region. This landform is also home to the famed Muir Woods National Monument.

Mount Tamalpais Park is just south of the Muir Woods. Within this park, at the top of a small hill, is a stone outcrop that was once a place of great power to the Miwok Indians. The site of these natural stones, arranged in a somewhat circular fashion, was a place where Miwoks would come to worship. Early explorers reported great gatherings at this spot. Unfortunately, by the time scholars decided to ask questions, most of the traditions had been lost or forgotten. All we have today are the remnants of old tales and sparse gleanings of activity that once took place.

The Miwoks lived along the Pacific Coast between San Francisco and Monterey. They built conical grass-covered houses atop the high rugged hills. There's an intriguing myth associated with the Miwoks. It seems a hideous monster once plagued these people. According to legends it lived along the coast, crawling up from the ocean to any high spot. The monster would scan the countryside looking for Miwok children to devour. This devilish scourge plagued the people until the trickster, Coyote, overpowered the monster.

Near the top of Mount Tamalpais one has a commanding view of the region. Known locally as the Flight Stones because of their use as a launching point for hang gliders, the stones are said to exhibit strange magnetic properties. On two separate occasions while I visited the site, my Sunto pocket compass needle fluctuated wildly after I stepped near the stones. Instead of pointing toward magnetic north, the needle at first slowly spun in a clockwise direction. As I moved around the stones, the rate of spinning increased. Upon my moving away from the outcrop, the needle returned to its regular course. This is peculiar, for on a third trip to the site nothing unusual happened—no strange magnetic variations, no visions, nothing.

The lack of consistency at the site with respect to compass needles must give one pause. The essence of science is duplicability—one must be able to duplicate an experiment's results with reliability and consistency. The fact that the needle moved erratically two out of three times is intriguing but disappointing in scientific terms. Other researchers have come up with similar confusing results.

But perhaps this is not that unusual, for the outcrop sits above the San Andreas Fault. Some have suggested that the incredible tension and pressure of two continental plates rubbing against each other somehow influences the earth's magnetic pull. Is it possible that the compass needle was responding to slight variations within the fault system? Is it possible that the Miwok Indians used this place because they experienced something otherworldly here? Perhaps they were sensitive to the mysterious forces emanating from deep within the earth. If so, this would explain much about this mysterious place.

Contact Persons and Organizations

Muir Woods National Monument
Mill Valley, CA 94941
(415) 388-2595

California Division of Mines and Geology, Information and Publications
1516 9th Street
Sacramento, CA 95814
(916) 445-1825

California Division of Mines and Geology, Division Headquarters
801 K Street
Sacramento, CA 95814
(916) 445-5716

California Mining Journal
P.O. Box 2260, 9011 Soquel Drive
Aptos, CA 95001
(408) 662-2899
Fax: (408) 662-3014

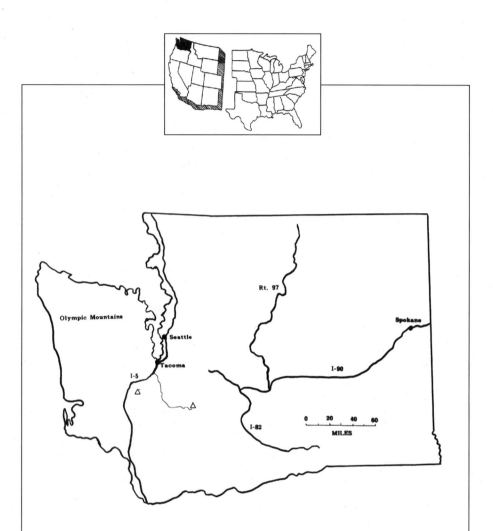

Mysterious Sites in Washington

7

Washington

Washington is a state in complicated geological transition. A large portion of the massive Pacific Plate is sliding underneath the entire state. Evidence of this is the line of volcanoes making up the Cascade Mountains. The explosion of Mount St. Helens is only the most recent upheaval in this geologically active area.

West-Central Washington

The area from Tacoma on the coast to Mount Rainier inland consists of thousands of feet of glacial debris. When the last glacier melted, millions of tons of soil and boulders that had been locked in the ice flowed freely, sometimes leaving deposits over two thousand feet deep in the Tacoma region.

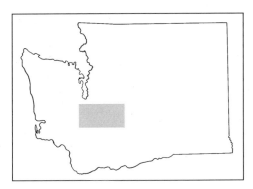

This part of Washington is filled with evidence of ancient mudflows and violent volcanic activity. It is also the most populated part of the state. The reason for the striking beauty of the Pacific Northwest is due to violent volcanic activity that continues to the present day. Volcanoes are merely vents for the chaos below the earth.

The Pacific Northwest is an accident waiting to happen. The earth's crust underneath this beautiful region is being twisted, shoved, and distorted in ways that we can't imagine. Whenever there's an earthquake in Alaska or California, the people in the Seattle region worry. Their state is situated along the vast continental and Pacific plates.

MIMA MOUNDS
Tenino, Washington

Site Synopsis

In a field just off Route 507 outside of Tenino are hundreds of dimplelike mounts approximately four feet in diameter by three feet in height. Controversy has raged ever since they were first noticed in the nineteenth century by Pacific Northwest pioneers. While superficially resembling smaller versions of the burial mounds found throughout the Ohio and Mississippi Valleys of the American heartland, excavation of these mounds has shown that they are naturally forming ground "bumps." How did this geological anomaly form?

Location

From Seattle's SeaTac Airport, head south on I-5 for approximately sixty-five miles, passing through Tacoma and Olympia until you reach the town of Essex. At Essex, travel northeast toward Tenino for eight miles. This road links up with Route 507 at Tenino.

Considerations

Almost all of the mounds are on private land. Permission from the landowner *must* be obtained before walking on any mound property.

History/Background

The origin of the Mima Mounds has been a mystery since the

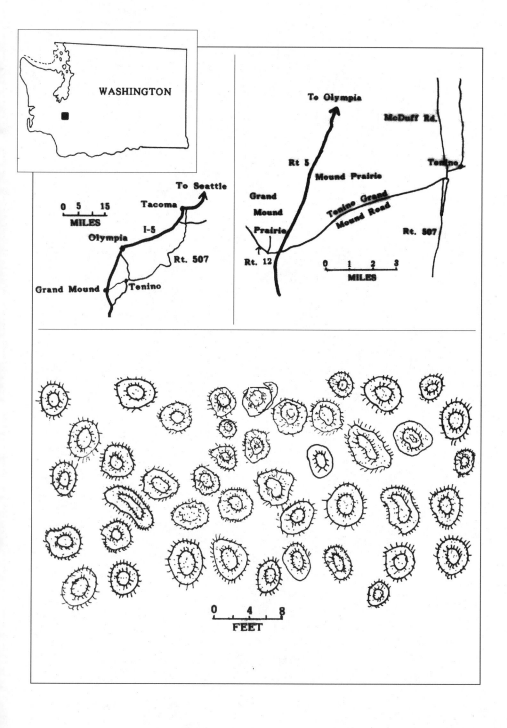

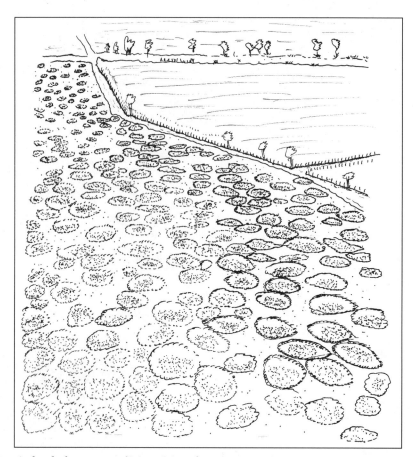

A sketched overview of Mima Mounds.

first report of their existence, in the early 1800s. In July 1842, Commander Charles Wilkes traveled to the region south of Olympia, Washington, and dug into the mounds. He concluded that "they bear the marks of savage labor, and are such an undertaking as they would have required the united efforts of a whole tribe."[1]

Over the next one hundred years, a variety of researchers has tried to solve the mystery. In the 1850s two naturalists working on a railroad survey suggested that a "giant root" caused the mounds. By 1871 a University of California geologist tried to show the mounds were caused by the peculiar conditions of surface erosion.

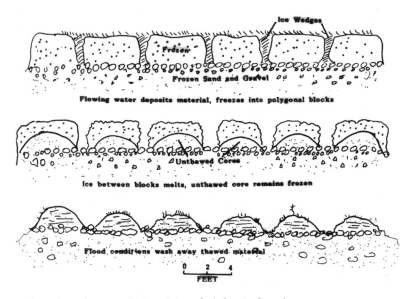

A hypothetical origin of Mima Mounds (after Jackson).

Later, everything from ants to giant gophers were said to be responsible for the strange cluster of mounds.

In 1956, a soil scientist writing in *Natural History* magazine summarized the most current explanations for the Mima Mounds.[2] According to various geologists, the mounds were the remains of buckled blocks of frozen ground. As the earth thawed, irregular blocks of ground eroded first at the upper levels, resulting in a rounded form (because the edges melt away more rapidly than the sides). The timing of frost and thaw was especially important for this to have happened thus.

While this seems to be the most logical explanation, it nonetheless is still a mystery. Not everyone supports the frost/thaw hypothesis.

Contact Persons and Organizations

Good information on these pattern mounds can be found in the U.S. Geological Survey professional papers or in the *Bulletins* of the Washington Division of Geology and Resources, all found in major libraries. Another readily available source is Howard Jackson's article in *Natural History:* "The Mystery of the Mima Mounds," published in March 1956 (see the Bibliography).

MOUNT RAINIER
Mount Rainier National Park, Washington

Site Synopsis

It is impossible to live in the Seattle/Tacoma region of Washington State and not be influenced by the looming presence of Mount Rainier. There is one stretch of highway leading south from Seattle toward the Seattle/Tacoma Airport (SeaTac) where this ancient volcano dominates the horizon. It is an overwhelming sight, even for those who have grown up surrounded by 14,000-foot peaks in the Rocky Mountains. The reason is that Mount Rainier juts up alone above a relatively flat horizon.

Living in the shadow of potential natural violence must influence all who live in the vicinity. Furthermore, the incredible geological forces responsible for this fantastic presence lie just underneath the floor of the state.

Location

From Seattle, drive south on Interstate 5. Just past Tacoma, exit at Lakeview onto Route 167. In two and one-half miles, exit Route 167 onto Route 7. Travel onward for thirty-five miles to the town of Elbe. At Elbe, continue eastward on Route 706 for twenty-four miles to Paradise. There's a lovely ski lodge and information center at Paradise, as well as access to hiking trails.

Considerations

This is beautiful country; the vistas are powerful. But it serves one to remember that this is a volcano. The 1980 eruption of Mount St. Helens some one hundred miles to the southeast was a surprise to hikers and campers in the region. Be prepared.

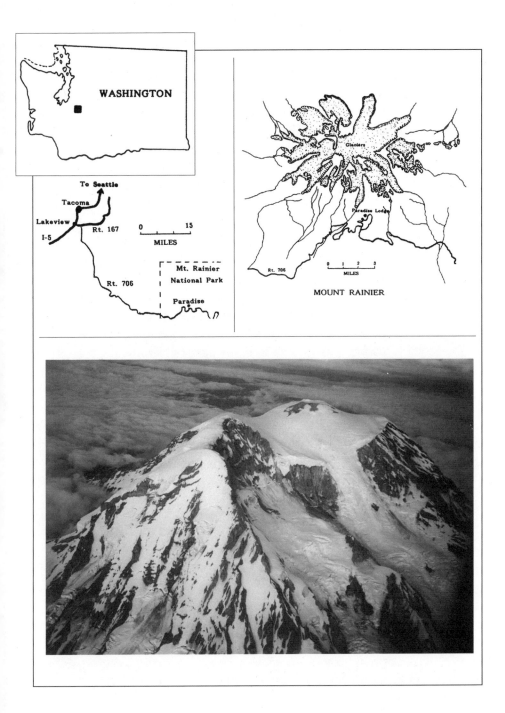

WASHINGTON

To Seattle

Tacoma

Lakeview

I-5

Rt. 167

0 15
MILES

Rt. 706

Mt. Rainier
National Park

Paradise

Glaciers

Paradise Lodge

Rt. 706

0 1 2 3
MILES

MOUNT RAINIER

On the highway, observe all posted speeds. The curving and narrow mountain roads demand special attention. If you encounter a bear, stay in your car and try to drive off. Bears are wild creatures and can be unpredictable and dangerous. Do not feed or approach them.

In the backcountry, hike only with others and be prepared for sudden weather changes. Carry your own shelter and stove. The many glaciers atop Mount Rainier contain deep hidden crevasses. Stay off them.

There are three types of camping in the wilderness of Mount Rainier National Park: trailside camps, crosscountry camping, and alpine camping. Each has its own set of rules and regulations. Contact the various hiking centers for details.

There are some general rules for people using the Mount Rainier backcountry:

- Anyone camping overnight in the park between June 15 and September 30, except in auto campgrounds, must obtain a backcountry permit from the park's superintendent.
- Dogs, cats, and other pets are not permitted in the backcountry. Leave them home.
- Fires are only permitted in special regions of the park.
- Party sizes may not exceed five people (unless it's an immediate family). Groups with permits may have trailside camps of up to twelve individuals.

History/Background

On a clear day, Mount Rainier looms over the western Washington area like a massive giant. It is a staggering sight. Rising 14,410 feet above sea level, this volcano began spewing lava over one million years ago. Geologists estimate that sometime around seventy-five thousand years ago it reached its maximum height before the scouring onslaught of the Ice Age.

Mount Rainier was a sacred site to the Pacific Northwest Indians. Known as *Takhoma*, it was the focal point of many vision quests. It's not hard to understand why, for on a clear day one can see the peak's snowfields from a distance of over one hundred miles.

The volcano is still very active. Over twenty-five hundred years ago, hot lava poured down toward the Seattle region. Sometime around five hundred years ago, massive outpourings of pumice killed most of the trees near the base of Rainier. Newspaper reporters in the Seattle region some one hundred years ago reported seeing fire and smoke from the mountain. As recently as the 1970s, steam explosions were tracked near the summit of the mountain. One explosion caused a major rockfall.

Cataclysmic eruptions are part of the life of volcanoes. Could Mount Rainier blow up today? Sure. And the spewing of hot rock would not be the only result. Perhaps more devastating would be the enormous mud flows that would ensue. Molten magma would quickly melt the snowfields and glaciers atop the mountain. The rush of melted water would scoop up billions of tons of mountainside and send it cascading toward level ground. The mind-boggling devastation caused by melting ice along the valleys of Mount St. Helens in 1980 should give us pause.

The obvious question is, If this is so, then how can people continue living in such a potentially dangerous area? How can anyone look up at the mountain on a clear morning and not be frightened? Collective disregard is the answer. Since an eruption hasn't happened in recent times, most people conveniently don't think about it. They go on about their daily lives, buying milk, driving their cars, paying their bills, as if their environment was the most humdrum and stable around.

This is classic denial. But there is an edge that comes from living in the face of overwhelming danger. The Neapolitans in Italy, who live at the base of Mount Vesuvius, the same volcano that wiped out Pompeii in A.D. 71, have a certain cavalier attitude toward all they do: work hard, play very hard, for tomorrow you may die. There's a frantic tension in the air that's probably born of two thousand years of inhabiting a dangerous area. There's a delicious edge to these people and all that goes on in Naples, a tumultuous nervousness to get on with life and forget about tomorrow.

Does one detect the same edge in the people in the Seattle region? Not readily. Most who live there are jaded by the blandness of American popular culture—the enclosed shopping malls, the familiar national restaurant chains—so one tends not to see this nervousness in most. Or maybe it's just masked. People closer to the edge, for example those not trapped by mortgages, bills, health-care funding, feel it. Teenagers in the area feel it. Musicians express it with their music the same way Neapolitans express it in their faces. Living above a continental plate's rim near a volcano that could erupt at any moment makes one appreciate the present in a way that's difficult for people who live in more stable environs to understand. Mount Rainier is indeed a strange and weird place to visit.

Contact Persons and Organizations

Mount Rainier National Park was established in 1899 and is administered by the National Park Service, U.S. Department of the Interior. The superintendent of the park can be reached at: Ashland, WA 98304; (206) 569-2211. Or for more general information, contact: Mount Rainier National Park, Tahoma Woods, Star Route, Ashford, WA 98304; (202) 569-2211.

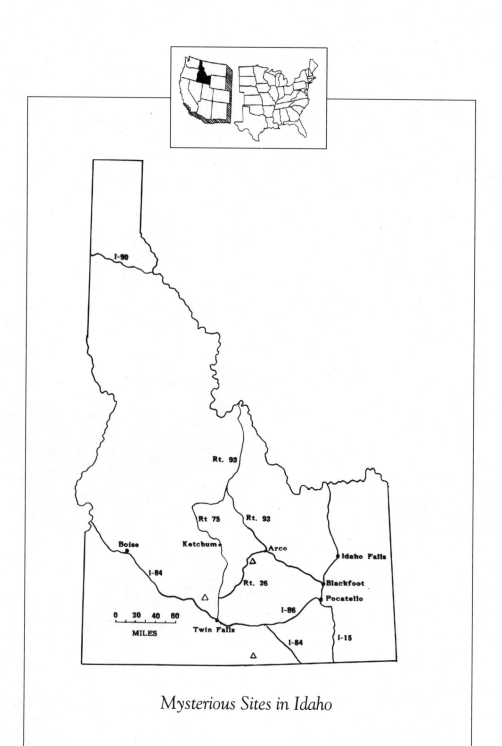

Mysterious Sites in Idaho

8

Idaho

The geology of Idaho is complicated. The state has been twisted, crushed, moved, pulled, and gnawed at for millions of years. The western boundary was at one time a beachfront. Large sections of this area are missing crucial bedrock. Geologists speculate the missing rocks somehow floated off to Siberia, Australia, or some point in between. Giant rifts scar the region and have left evidence of massive volcanic upheaval. Dramatic, impossible things happened in this place.

Around 60 million years ago, the climate changed. First there was a long dry spell, then Idaho became tropical, with lush forests covering the mountains for a few million years. And then came the ice. Geologists speculate that multiple ice ages crept across Idaho. The effects of the last two, however, are most noticeable. The bulldozer effect of massive ice walls widened the burgeoning river valleys. When the glaciers melted, Idaho's streams began to flow. The landscape of craggy high peaks and jagged mountains we see today is the direct result of the last glacial meltdown, which occurred some ten thousand years ago.

Southern Idaho

This part of Idaho consists of broad basins made of ancient lava flows, upthrust faults, and sedimentary deposition. The Albion Range, of which the Silent City of Rocks is part, was twisted and contorted when the Rocky Mountains first compressed and had their beginnings. Ten million years ago, the eruptions in the region around Yellowstone in Wyoming blanketed the area with lava. Rivers and erosion have since cut through, exposing rock some 600 million years old.

The southern part of Idaho was long part of a trail leading to the West, for there is a continuation there of the gradual pass through the Rocky Mountains.

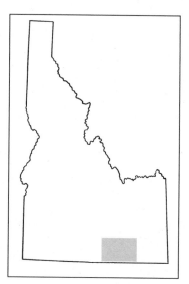

SILENT CITY OF ROCKS
West of Almo, Idaho

Site Synopsis

Along the southern range of mountains west of Almo in southern Idaho are a maze of weirdly carved granite erosions. Scattered over a nine-square-mile area are clusters of extraordinary eroded rock forms that look like little villages. First surveyed in the 1930s but known long before by countless tribes of indigenous Americans, these curious granite outcrops have long impressed and frightened travelers to the region.

Location

From Idaho Falls, travel south on I-15. At Pocatello, travel southwest on I-86. Exit at Burley, taking Route 27 south to Oakley.

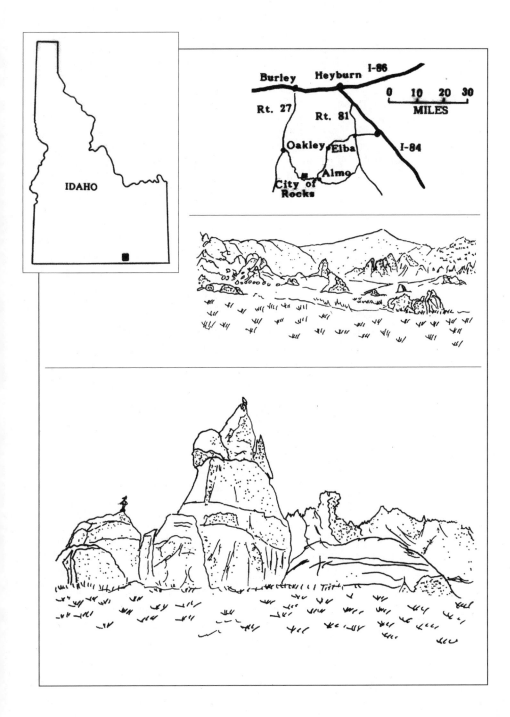

Continue southeastward from Oakley for ten miles. Watch for the signs that say City of Rocks National Reserve.

Considerations

Care must be taken not to stray from trails. Please do not climb about on the eroded rocks: They are fragile. Also, watch for granite slabs that have eroded too quickly and too much.

Leave all artifacts, stones, and the like in place!

History/Background

This silent windswept cluster of rocks was once bustling with traffic. It was a famous landmark along the Oregon Trail—the five-hundred-mile pathway across the Rockies—that led pioneers from Missouri to the Oregon Territory. At this famous landmark the trail split, and one path went on toward California. Pioneers inscribed their names on many of the rock spires in axle grease.

The mass of granite here is over fifty million years old. During that enormous time period it has eroded into a fantasy land of spires, natural bridges, animal shapes, hollow boulders, and "bathtub" rocks. Granite naturally erodes into weird shapes, but because of a variety of factors the granite here has eroded into delicate forms that to the untrained eye seem purposeful. Resistant quartzite caps many of the granite domes. This, coupled with the odd fractures and cleavages within the granite, has allowed for slow, uneven erosion and weathering. The results are turrets, fortresses, towers, and other extraordinary assemblages of natural forms.

This place is a must-see, especially at sunset. One can almost hear the early pioneers laughing and grunting along on their quest for a better life.

Scattered at the base of these granite forms are innumerable Indian artifacts: points, broken polishing stones, bits of pottery. The large number of surface finds suggests that this site was well visited in prepioneer days. We can only guess why the site was popular among the indigenous population of southern Idaho: Spirits clearly inhabited this special place!

Contact Persons and Organizations

City of Rocks
(208) 678-7230

The best description of this site can be found in the first survey of the region. While difficult to obtain in most local libraries, it can easily be ordered via an interlibrary loan: Alfred L. Anderson. "Geology and Mineral Resources of Eastern Cassia County, Idaho," *Idaho Bureau of Mines and Geology Bulletin*, no. 14 (September 1931).

LITTLE CITY OF ROCKS
Gooding, Idaho

Site Synopsis

Grotesque, naturally eroded rock sculptures grace eight valleys.

Location

From Gooding, take Route 46 north for twelve and one-half miles. Turn left onto a dirt road at a sign pointing west. Travel along this road for a mile.

Considerations

If hiking in the summertime, bring lots of water and a snack.

History/Background

Several million years ago, volcanoes in the area spewed out millions of tons of pale, dense granitelike ash known as *rhyolite*. In the ensuing years, some parts of the ash became more complicated than others. The action of wind and rain has eroded away the softer rhyolite, leaving the more resistant ash standing in weird formations.

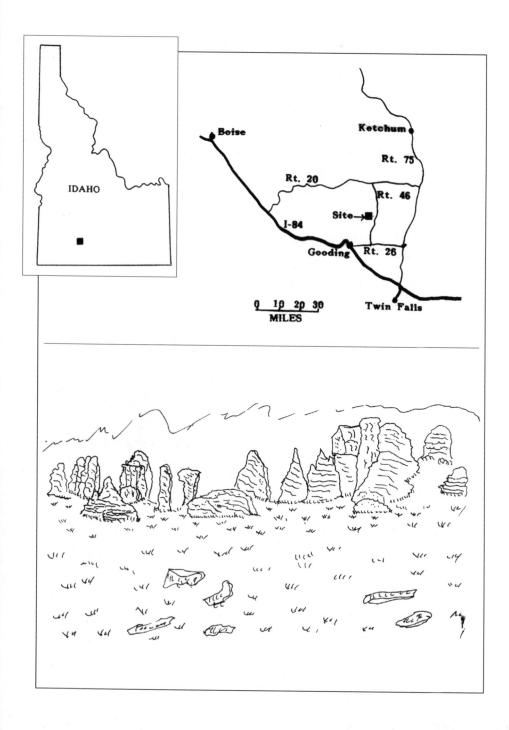

Although it's not as well known as the rock city west of Almo, this site allows for some intriguing hikes through a total of eight canyons. While this is difficult to arrange, this place is best appreciated on a clear night during a full moon.

Contact Persons and Organizations

Idaho Geological Survey
Bureau of Mines and Geology
University of Idaho
Moscow, ID 83843

THE GREAT RIFT
Craters of the Moon National Monument, southwest of Arco, Idaho

Site Synopsis

Open fissures rip across the Snake River plain of southeastern Idaho.

Location

From Pocatello, drive south on I-86 to American Falls. Cross the Snake River bridge, traveling north Route 37 toward Aberdeen. Watch for signs leading to the Great Rift National Landmark.

Considerations

Be very careful when looking down into the dark fissures of the Great Rift. Some drop down over eight hundred feet!

Bring along a flashlight to explore the so-called Indian Tunnel—a rather large lava tube where Native Americans built rock shelters for hunting parties.

History/Background

Southwest of Arco along Route 20 is an eerie place that early

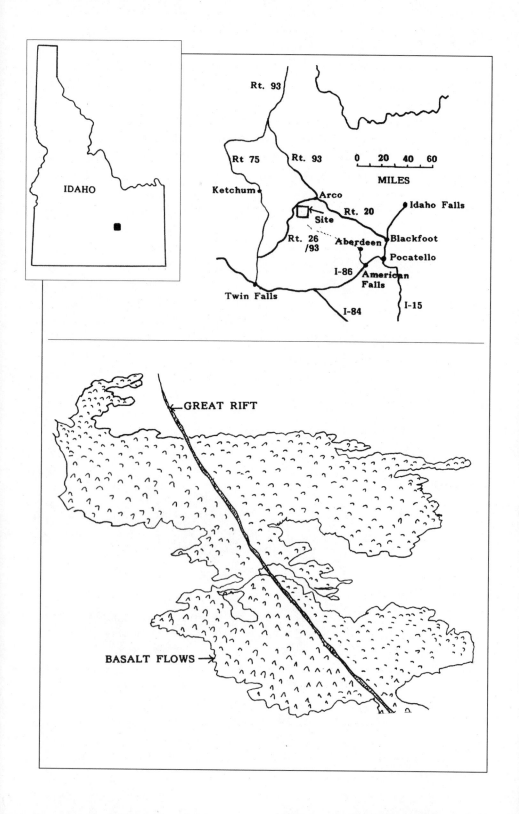

pioneers made a point to avoid. The pleasant sagebrush terrain changes quickly into a desolate "moonscape." Volcanoes have spewed up large amounts of lava in this area, and cinder cone mountains abound. The lava here changes color from black to red, and much of it is angular and dangerous.

South of Craters of the Moon National Monument are several ten- to twenty-mile-long tears in the earth. Over the past several thousand years or so, the movement of the earth's crust has ripped it open to expose dark, open fissures across the entire eastern Snake River plain. At the Craters of the Moon site, black basalt has oozed up from the depths of the rift, spilling out onto the plain and solidifying into massive dark patches.

This entire area is spooky, for the basaltic flows occurred not millions of years ago but only thousands of years ago. The deep fissures found along this plain allow us to begin to comprehend the power of continental plate movement. This site is much younger than the Questa and Taos Rift. But in time it will become as wide and deep as the New Mexican rift.

Some people claim they sense pulses of energy at the rift sites that feel similar to getting a shock from walking across a carpet. A few say they've seen weird greenish lights glowing near the fissures. Although I've never seen the light or been shocked at the rifts, there is data suggesting that massive movements of the earth's crust somehow generates photon emissions—pulses of light. Anecdotes from earthquake survivors report flashes of green on the distant horizon prior to a quake. Maybe there's something to this.

Contact Persons and Organizations

Craters of the Moon National Monument
P.O. Box 29
Arco, ID 83213
(208) 527-3257, -3207

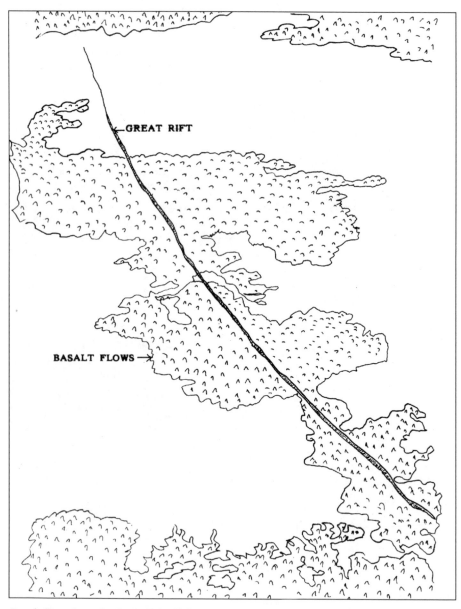

Basalt flows from the Great Rift, Idaho.

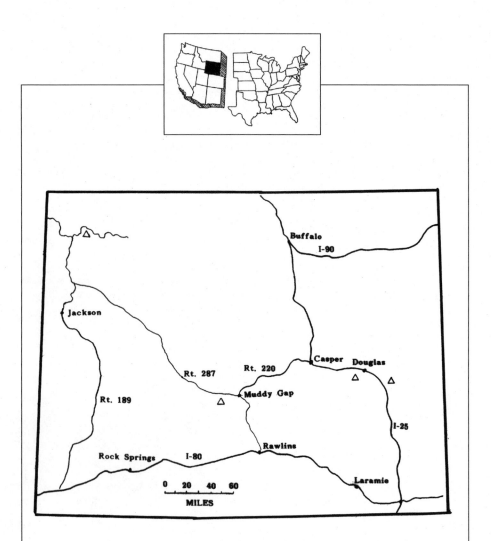

Mysterious Sites in Wyoming

9

Wyoming

Wyoming can be divided into two parts. The western section contains the Rocky Mountains, while the eastern section is part of the Great Plains. Various north-south mountain ranges punctuate the state.

East-Central Wyoming

Beautiful desolation is the best way to describe eastern Wyoming. Long sweeping vistas of gently rolling prairie are occasionally broken up by the odd hillock or butte. As one travels east from Casper along Interstate 25, huge ranches with black Angus cattle seem to go on forever. The terrain is the result of an ancient inland sea that once covered much of the central United States some 300 million years ago.

AYRES NATURAL BRIDGE
Converse County, Wyoming

Site Synopsis

Tucked up against the foothills of the Medicine Bow Mountains is a natural sandstone bridge. The bridge arches fifty feet above a flowing creek and is one hundred feet long. There's a story that Indians in the area avoided the place due to a powerful evil spirit that lived below the arch. There is documentation to support this. Travelers fleeing over the plains who made it to the arch were safe: Indians refused to follow. Why should this be?

Location

From Casper, travel fifty miles east along I-25. At the Natural Bridge interchange—exit 151—turn off onto County Road 13. Proceed along this road for five miles. Drive slowly and carefully, because the road bends and dips, creating many blind spots. Follow the signs toward the arch. Drive past the caretaker's house toward the camping area and park there. Walk across the footbridge toward the arch.

Considerations

Ayres Natural Bridge is part of the Converse County, Wyoming, Park and Recreation Division. There are several rules to abide by. The bridge site is open from April through October, 8:00 A.M. to 8:00 P.M. Throwing rocks or taking any type of artifact from the site is prohibited. Look but leave everything in place! Leave your pistol or rifle in the car.

History/Background

Ayres Natural Bridge is one of the few natural bridges in the world that has water flowing under it. It was formed from the erosive action of wind and water that has allowed LaPrele Creek to expand and open the initially small hole in the sandstone.

The bridge is part of a rock strata known locally as the Casper Sandstone Formation. More than three hundred million years ago this part of Wyoming was covered by a vast inland sea that stretched from the Gulf of Mexico all the way into Canada. When that sea began to dry up, the beaches around the water began to lose their moisture and settle. Millions of years of windblown debris covered this sand, compacting it into hard rock.

The bridge arch is set in a gorgeous amphitheater of one hundred-foot red standstone walls with many shade trees. A walk along the canyon walls will reveal many inscriptions from previous visitors from the mid-1800s to the present.

The bridge is a few miles south of the Oregon Trail. In the early 1840s, one of the great migrations in recorded history began with the opening of the trail. From 1843 to 1869 (with completion of the transcontinental railroad), over 350,000 pioneers led covered wagons along this 487-mile-long road. Starting in Independence, Missouri, and ending in "Oregon Country," these pioneers were the start of the great westward migration and eventual expansion of United States territory to the Pacific Ocean.

The trail was first forged by fur trappers who were employed to seek out fertile beaver streams. The trail, which goes right through the center of Wyoming, was the route of choice of these intrepid explorers and of later pioneer settlers, for several reasons. It had a steady supply of good water and a dependable supply of grass for their cattle; but the route also provided the only passable grade over the Rocky Mountains. Wagon trains could travel over it with no problems whatsoever. In a sense, the state of Wyoming exists due to its favorable pasture, water, and this route over the mountains.

It is difficult to imagine anyone avoiding this place. It is an idyllic oasis amid a sea of desolate prairie. There is the shelter of the red sandstone, a ready source of water, shade trees, and an easily defensible narrow entranceway into the alcove. There must have been powerful reasons why the Shoshone refused to follow white settlers into the amphitheater. Perhaps they were aware of things that we know nothing of.

In 1882, Alva Ayres, an early traveler in the region, settled on land that included the bridge. By the early 1920s his family deeded

Mysterious circular and twisted tubular formations in stone at the base of Ayres Natural Bridge.

the land on which the bridge is located to Converse County. Eventually, the county turned it into a day park.

When visiting this site, don't be put off by the picnic tables and play areas. The site is mysterious for several reasons. Look past its graceful beauty and get up close to the base of the arch. At eye level you will see hundreds of circular and twisting tubular formations in the stone. Closer inspection reveals that these formations, scattered along the lowest level of the arch, are concretions. Over millions of years minerals have deposited around "seed" nodules within the sandstone. Thin sections of tiny spheres that have fallen off the arch through erosion reveal the nucleus around which stone has formed. But there is more.

Examine the debris surrounding the creek. If you are careful you will see clumps of fossil jaws and teeth. These are the remains of ancient herd animals that ran through this country over one million years ago. Some of the remnants are hideous. Perhaps this is the origin of the King of Beasts legend of the Indians.

The indigenous Indians throughout the West were skilled stone workers. They had an eye for all kinds of stone and were expert craftsmen who manipulated rock as if it were clay. These people were also skilled in animal anatomy—their very existence depended upon their ability to utilize all parts of a killed animal. They certainly saw these peculiar spheres and stone jaws and teeth. To find an animal jaw of massive proportions and made of stone must have been puzzling to them. Could they have seen evil things associated with these findings? Perhaps the thought of the spirits of these strange and unusual creatures frightened them and led them to avoid the arch.

Contact Persons and Organizations

An excellent book on the general geology of Wyoming is David R. Lageson and Darwin R. Spearing's *Roadside Geology of Wyoming* (Missoula, Mont.: Mountain Press Publishing Co., 1988).

The Wyoming Pioneer Memorial Museum
Center Street, Wyoming State Fairgrounds
P.O. Drawer 10
Douglas, WY 82633
(307) 358-9288

The Geological Survey of Wyoming
P.O. Box 3008, University Station
Laramie, WY 82071
(307) 745-4495

Wyoming Geological Association
P.O. Box 545
Casper, WY 82602
(307) 237-0027

SPANISH DIGGINGS
South of Manville, Wyoming

Site Synopsis

Along a region of low sloping hills, covering an area of approximately ten by forty miles, are hundreds of aboriginal stone-quarry
sites. For thousands of years Native Americans came here to pry
out of the rock face core stones that would eventually become arrowheads, spear points, knives, and scrapers. One site twenty miles
south of Manville is accessible to the traveler.

Location

From Casper, travel east on I-25 toward Douglas. A few miles
past Douglas is Route 18/20. Take this road east toward Manville.
At the Route 270 junction, turn south. The road leading to the
Spanish Diggings site is 19.3 miles south of the Route 18/20 and
Route 270 junction. After 19.3 miles (2.3 miles south of the
Glendo Reservoir turnoff sign) there's a nondescript white road
leading east into the hills. Drive 2.7 miles on this road. At the end
of this distance, on your left, you'll see an eroded rock overhang
and an intermittent streambed. Pull off the road and walk west
along the streambed. There are several examples of Indian excavations here. Watch for evidence of the ancients.

Considerations

The white-dirt path leading to the diggings can be treacher-
ous. There are several quick turns and dips along the way. Heavy
trucks also use this road, so proceed carefully. When walking
through the streambeds please look, but don't touch what you
see.

History/Background

The mountains making up these sites attracted the attention
of prehistoric indigenous peoples thousands of years ago because a

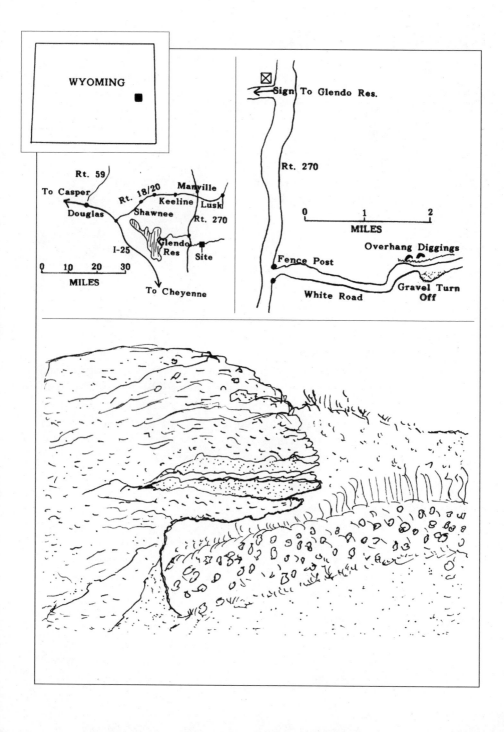

WYOMING

Rt. 59
To Casper
Rt. 18/20   Manville
Douglas   Keeline Lusk
Shawnee   Rt. 270
I-25   Glendo
            Res   Site
0   10   20   30
MILES
To Cheyenne

Sign To Glendo Res.

Rt. 270

0   1   2
MILES

Overhang Diggings
Fence Post
White Road   Gravel Turn
                  Off

certain type of stone is exposed here. Fine-grained flint, chert, and samples of obsidian can all be found scattered throughout the mountain range. Geologically, these mountains were *the* source for tribes ranging all the way to the Great Plains. White settlers coming into Wyoming's east-central district noticed these quarry sites and assumed they were evidence of the early Spanish Conquistadors' obsessive search for gold, hence the name.

Walking through the streambeds here and elsewhere along this vast region of source rock, it is easy to understand the area's attraction. Good-quality cutting and grinding stone abounds in nice discrete chunks. Based on the size of the diggings and artifacts found at several sites, the quarries may have been continuously used for over five thousand years. Being in the presence of such ancient work is a little overwhelming. But the region is mysterious for other reasons as well.

Depending on the season and time of day, one can drive for miles and see not another vehicle, building, or any other indication of human existence save for an occasional windmill. While this phenomena is nothing new to westerners who have grown up in areas where the closest house is one hundred miles down the road, it is unnerving to almost everyone else. One must be very sure of one's vehicle when driving in this country. If you run out of gas or snap a fan belt it might be hours or even days before another car comes along! Furthermore, the terrain speaks of the ancients. This is a land that saw much human activity for a long time. When the sun is setting and a full moon rising, one can almost feel the blood, sweat, and tears of the people who came here to work. The place has a somewhat creepy feeling that is probably the result of the combination of desolation, rocky terrain, and evidence of ancient activity. Tread carefully over this mysterious area.

And finally, if any of the UFO abduction accounts of drivers on lonely roads encountering aliens are true, then Route 270 south of Manville is the perfect location for a galaxy-class starship to come swooping down. Whenever I've traveled that road during dusk in search of more "Spanish Diggings," I've always had the oddest sensation that *something* around or above was observing my every move. Perhaps it was fatigue that played with my mind. Or perhaps something else. . .

Contact Persons and Organizations

The Wyoming Pioneer Memorial Museum
Center Street, Wyoming State Fairgrounds
P.O. Drawer 10
Douglas, WY 82633
(307) 358-9288

The Geological Survey of Wyoming
P.O. Box 3008, University Station
Laramie, WY 82071
(307) 745-4495

Wyoming Geological Association
P.O. Box 545
Casper, WY 82602
(307) 237-0027

West-Central Wyoming

The region just south of Crooks and neighboring Green Mountain is a high desert called the Great Divide Basin. This is essentially a low-sloping area that drains onto itself and not to either ocean. This is a harsh, dry, and barren land regardless of the presence of elk and mule deer, which are common in the sloping mountains.

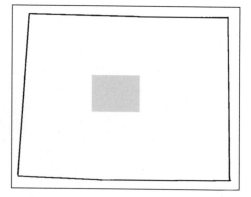

The prevalence of oil wells throughout the Crooks Range suggests that millions of years ago the climate of this region was much different than it is today.

A nineteenth-century illustration of the Sweet Water (central) region of Wyoming. (Reprinted from Vivian, Wanderings)

GIANT CONGLOMERATES OF CROOKS MOUNTAIN
Central Wyoming

Site Synopsis

Crooks Mountain in central Wyoming is composed of sixty-five-million-year-old conglomerates more than one thousand feet in thickness. Granite boulders from five to ten feet in diameter are piled one on top of another. The boulders, some weighing more than one thousand tons, increase in size from the bottom toward the top of the succession!

Location

Getting to this mountain takes time and energy. Travel southwest on Route 220 from Casper for seventy-two miles before the road continues west as Route 287/789. Continue for another

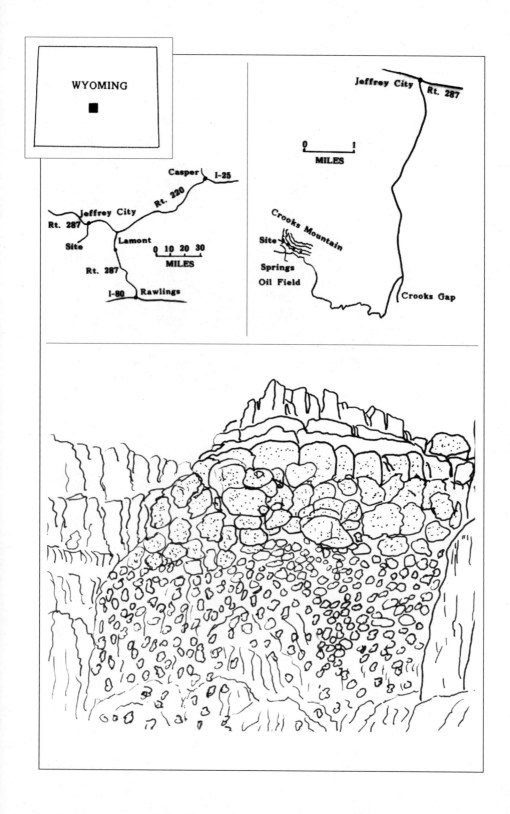

WYOMING

Casper I-25

Rt. 220

Jeffrey City

Rt. 287

Site   Lamont

Rt. 287   0 10 20 30
                MILES

I-80 Rawlings

Jeffrey City Rt. 287

0   1
MILES

Crooks Mountain

Site

Springs

Oil Field

Crooks Gap

twenty miles until you reach Jeffrey City. Proceed south for nine and one-half miles. At that point, look for a road going west. Turn onto this road and travel for another six miles. Crooks Mountain will be north of the road. Park along the base of the mountain and look up!

Considerations

Much of the land here is privately owned. Watch for posted signs and barbed wire fences. Most people in the town of Bairoil can tell you who owns what land. Take the time to get permission to walk the land.

History/Background

Due to some violent uplifts of land along a fault system around 1.8 billion years ago, Crooks Mountain is exposed with little weathering. It was covered over for much of its "life" until around 20 million years ago, when it was pushed up and folded. Twenty million years apparently hasn't caused much wear on this staggeringly ancient mountain.

The Oregon Trail blazed its way across this section of Wyoming, for the terrain here allowed passage through the spine of the Rockies by its low, sloping character.

Usually large boulders settle to the bottom of a mountain pile. The reason for the larger boulders on top of smaller boulders here has to do with the uplifting phenomena some twenty million years ago. This site is intriguing for its age.

Contact Persons and Organizations

An excellent book on the general geology of Wyoming is David R. Lageson and Darwin R. Spearing's *Roadside Geology of Wyoming* (Missoula, Mont.: Mountain Press Publishing Co., 1988).

The Geological Survey of Wyoming
P.O. Box 3008, University Station
Laramie, WY 82071
(307) 745-4495

Wyoming Geological Association
P.O. Box 545
Casper, WY 82602
(307) 237-0027

Northwest Wyoming

The northwest of Wyoming is what comes to mind most when people visualize the state. This is the region of the Grand Tetons, those majestic mountains that have inspired and spooked generations of mountain men and settlers.

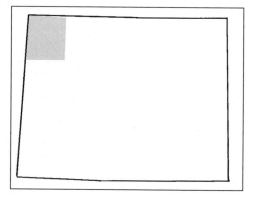

YELLOWSTONE LAKE WHISPERS
Yellowstone National Park, Wyoming

Site Synopsis

From high above Yellowstone Lake comes a mysterious unearthly sound that has captured the attention of all who have heard it. It's been described as the vibrating whine of a harp. One early researcher said, "The sound begins softly in the remote distance, draws rapidly near with louder and louder throbs of sound and then it dies away in the opposite distance—the whole passage lasting from a few seconds to half a minute or more."[1]

Some have tried to explain the phenomena in terms of wind blowing through the surrounding peaks or even volcanic tension deep within the earth.

Location

From Rock Springs, take Route 191 north for 180 miles to Jackson. At Jackson, continue on Route 191. In a few miles the

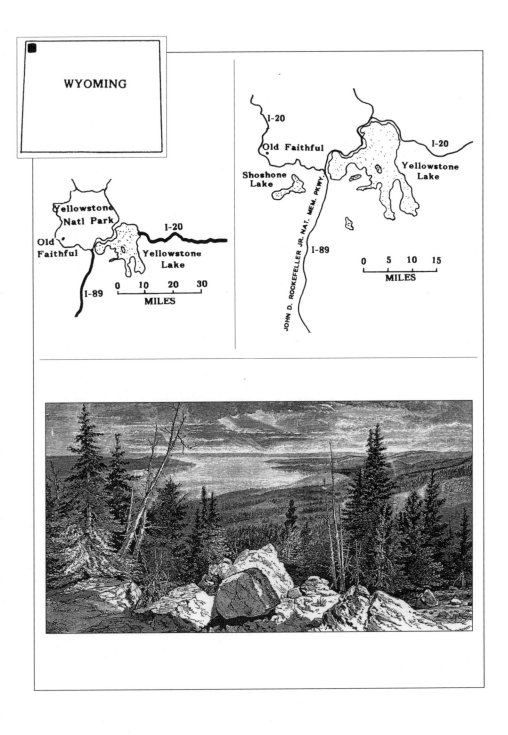

road will combine Route 26, Route 191, and I-89. Continue on I-89—the John D. Rockefeller Jr. National Memorial Parkway—for another eighty miles before reaching West Thumb Junction. From here, excursions can be taken to see Shoshone Lake. Another twenty miles brings one to Lake Junction.

Considerations

Yellowstone Lake is part of the National Park system. It is part of Yellowstone National Park, and one must abide by all park rules. No trash should be left in the park; there is no bear feeding and no climbing about where warnings are posted.

There are *many* intriguing things to see in this grandest of national parks. Aside from the obvious geothermal phenomena—Old Faithful is the most famous—there are scores of backcountry trails and rivers to explore.

To hear the whispers it is necessary to be at the park when few people are around. The summer season—starting in June and ending the first week of September—is not the time to travel to Yellowstone. It is the most visited national park in the country. Getting a motel room, if one has not been booked in advance, can be impossible! Furthermore, you will be frustrated by the numbers of campers chugging along high pass roads. If possible, visit the lake in late spring or early fall.

All reports state that the sound is fleeting and sudden, lasting around fifteen to thirty seconds. People usually hear it from just after sunrise to around 10:00 A.M., when the lake is calm and after a cool night. Several early explorers described it as sounding like a swarm of humming bees with a metallic twang.

The sound has been heard no farther west than nearby Shosone Lake or farther east than Yellowstone Lake, and not north or south of either of these lakes.

History/Background

Yellowstone Park was first explored in 1808 by John Colter, a member of the Lewis and Clark Expedition. When Lewis and Clark finished their journey in 1806, they met two trappers mov-

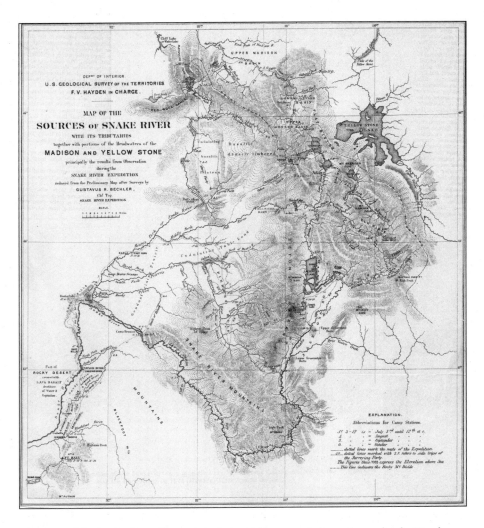

"Sources of the Snake River," a map depicting Yellowstone Lake as drawn by the Hayden Expedition in 1872. (Reprinted from Hayden, Sixth Annual Report)

ing upriver. They convinced one of them, John Colter, to guide them into the wilderness. A year later, after descending the Missouri River once again, he met other men who convinced him to return to the high mountains. One gets the impression that Colter didn't think too highly of early nineteenth-century American civilization.

Sometime during this second expedition, Colter went on a solitary journey into northwest Wyoming. Colter reported seeing "Hidden fires, smoking pits, noxious streams, and the all-pervading smell of brimstone," near the headwaters of Yellowstone River. The jokes were many. Few believed him. "Colter's Hell" was thought to be the result of his spending too many years in the wilderness alone. Clearly, however, he saw the many examples of geothermal activity in and around Yellowstone.

Mountain men and fur trappers long heard the sound emanating from Yellowstone Lake. Before them, many groups of Indians reported the lake talking. For them, great spirits lived in the vicinity. It is easy to understand why, with the staggering array of "fire and brimstone" in the region.

One of the first scientific reports of the phenomena comes from a Mr. F. H. Bradley, who wrote in F. V. Hayden's *Report for 1872 on Montana, Idaho, Wyoming and Utah*, that "While getting breakfast . . . we heard a hoarse whine, whose locality and character we could not at first determine. . . ."[2]

In 1893, Edwin Linton collected most of the accounts of this unearthly sound in an article for *Science*. He also gives his own account of the experience: "I heard a strange echoing sound in the sky, dying away to the southward, which appeared to me to be like a sound that had already been echoing some seconds before . . ."[3]

Linton questioned his mountain guides about the sound. Invariably they couldn't explain it, saying it was "the most mysterious sound heard among the mountains." The next morning, Linton, "heard the sound very plainly. It appeared to be directly overhead and to pass off across the sky, growing fainter and fainter towards the southwest . . . nearly everyone, in attempting to fix its location, turns his head to one side and glances upward."[4]

A few days later, Linton and his team "heard a sound overhead, like a rushing wind or like some invisible but comparatively dense body moving rapidly through the air and not very far above our heads."[5]

Most tellingly, this early researcher brings up an observation that flies in the face of the wind-across-the-mountains explanation:

> If this sound was produced by a current of air in motion overhead, it is difficult to understand why it did not give some account of itself, either in the clouds that were floating at different levels in the upper air or among the pines which covered the slope that rose more than 1,000 feet above our heads, or on the waters of the lake itself.[6]

So what is this sound that one hears during special moments at Yellowstone and Shoshone Lakes? It's very difficult to say. Recording ephemeral sounds is rather difficult, because they do not occur with any regularity. Hence, setting up complex recording equipment is great, but if the sound doesn't cooperate, one cannot analyze it. Perhaps this is good. Perhaps there are some things that need to be experienced firsthand. For the time being, at least, you need to be at these lakes early in the morning, and you also need to have the luck of the mountain gods to hear the sounds.

Prepare to be startled the first time you hear the "whispers." Your own description of the ethereal sound will depend on what mindset you bring to Yellowstone. I heard lilting bells wafting across a blue sky so gorgeous it hurt. Others hear wires snapping in the wind. To paraphrase an early explorer, the Yellowstone whispers are the most mysterious sounds in the mountains.

Contact Persons and Organizations

Yellowstone National Park
P.O. Box 168
Yellowstone National Park, WY 82190
(307) 344-7381

An excellent book on the general geology of Wyoming is David R. Lageson and Darwin R. Spearing's *Roadside Geology of Wyoming* (Missoula, Mont.: Mountain Press Publishing Co., 1988).

The Geological Survey of Wyoming
P.O. Box 3008, University Station
Laramie, WY 82071
(307) 745-4495

Wyoming Geological Association
P.O. Box 545
Casper, WY 82602
(307) 247-0027

10

Some Final Words

The eighteenth-century British statesman Edmund Burke wrote that "the passion caused by the great and sublime in nature . . . is astonishment; and astonishment is that state of the soul, in which all its emotions are suspended with some degree of horror." Or perhaps even terror.

Many of the sites described in this book span this range of emotion. Some are sublime: Lieutenant Ives's Colorado River journey and Ayers Canyon in Wyoming readily come to mind. Other places are terrifying, particularly late at night: the Little City of Rocks and the Craters of the Moon in Idaho are examples.

This book is the culmination of a long quest throughout the western states. The road has led to weird geology and strange ruins, some in the most desolate of areas. There's a mysterious world out there filled with extraordinary places.

The very fact that anomalies continue to be found is intriguing because it means that modern science has not explained everything. There's still a figurative world of spirits inhabiting the dark corners of the night. And while the last two hundred years of rationalism have done a superb job of describing everything from sand grains to mountains, the reality behind those descriptions continues to elude us. How, for instance, does a concretion form—and why? And why do some places on earth feel better than others?

The daily paradigms that each of us live with are satisfying and intellectually secure. It's nice to know the ground we walk upon is stable. But this artificial perspective doesn't include anomalies! Walking through the streets of New York, Denver, San Francisco, or any other city or town, it is easy to be

277

impressed by the artifacts of American civilization—the buildings, the roads, the imposing towers of twentieth-century life all suggest a high level of control of the environment. But step out into the Rocky Mountain West for a while. Remove yourself from the elecromagnetic flux of our society. Camp out near the Rio Grande Gorge under a nighttime sky that dazzles the senses with billions of stars stretching to the horizon, and suddenly the illusion of our "dominance" over the cosmos becomes evident. Listen to the Taos "hum"; gaze upon those inscribed cave slashes; drive for miles at sunset along lonely eastern Wyoming backroads and experience the sublime. It is easy to become overwhelmed by the unknown.

No doubt I've missed many locations that astonish local people—the West is a huge chunk of real estate. Feel free to contact me through my publisher if you stumble across some mysterious place. I can promise that I'll be up to see you in a flash.

As you set off to examine these strange, weird, and unusual sites, as you look upon odd crevices within the earth's crust, or as you contemplate the stream of sunlight entering a thousand-year-old Anasazi cave, keep in mind the musings of the English essayist and traveler William Hazlitt, who in 1826 wrote: "Nothing strikes the eye, nothing rivets the attention but ruins, the fragments of what has been. The past is like a halo forever surrounding and obscuring the present."

Notes

Chapter 1: History and Background

1. Jerome Wyckoff, *Rock Scenery of the Hudson Highlands and Palisades* (Glens Falls, N.Y.: Adirondack Mountain Club, 1971), 85.

2. John Finch, "On the Celtic Antiquities of America," *American Journal of Science* 7 (1824): 149-61.

3. Henriette Mertz, *Atlantis: Dwelling Place of the Gods* (Chicago: Private printing, 1976), 50, 52.

4. James Baldwin, *Ancient America in Notes on American Archaeology* (New York: Harper and Brothers, 1872), 43-44.

5. Ibid., 44.

6. Ibid., 45-46.

7. Mertz, *Atlantis*, 65.

8. Maurice Pope, *The Story of Archaeological Decipherment* (New York: Scribner, 1975), 7.

9. "Neolithic" indicates the "New Stone Age," when farming, semipermanent villages, and animal breeding displaced nomadic hunting.

10. Basque is an ancient, poorly understood language still spoken by the Basques, a people living in the northwestern Pyrenees on the Iberian Peninsula.

11. Andrew E. Rothovius, "The Celt-Culture of New England, First Millennium B.C.," *NEARA Journal* 10, no. 2 (Summer-Fall 1975).

12. Cyrus H. Gordon, *Before Columbus: Links Between the Old World and*

Ancient America (New York: Crown, 1971), 187.

13. Ibid., 145.

14. Henry Rowe Schoolcraft, *History of the Indian Tribes of the United States* (Philadelphia: J. B. Lippincott, 1857), 610.

Chapter 2: Colorado

1. Enrique Merino, "Self-Organization in Stylolites," *American Scientist* 80, no. 2 (September-October 1992): 466-73.

2. William R. McGlone and Phillip M. Leonard, *Ancient Celtic America* (Fresno, Calif.: Panorama West Books, 1986), 113.

3. Etienne Bernardeau Renaud, *Archaeological Survey of Eastern Colorado, 2nd Report* (Denver: University of Denver, 1931), 14.

4. Ibid., 12.

5. Ferdinand Vandeveer Hayden, *Tenth Annual Report of the United States Geological and Geographical Survey of the Territories embracing Colorado and Parts of Adjacent Territories Being a Report of Progress of the Exploration for the year 1876* (Washington, D.C.: Government Printing Office, 1878), 383.

Chapter 3: New Mexico

1. Edgar L. Hewett, *Pajarito Plateau and its Ancient People* (Albuquerque: University of New Mexico Press, 1938), 13.

2. Ibid., 14.

3. Brevet Lieutenant Colonel J. E. Johnston, et al., *Reports of the Secretary of War with Reconnaissances of Routes from San Antonio to El Paso*, 31st Cong., 1850, Ex. Doc. 64, 136-37.

4. Ibid., 77.

5. Ibid., 68.

6. Ibid., 134.

7. Ibid., 134.

8. Ibid., 83.

9. Ibid., 116.

10. Ibid., 83.

11. Ibid., 122.

12. Reader's Digest Association, *Earth's Mysterious Places* (Pleasantville, N.Y.: Reader's Digest Association, 1992), 18.

13. Stephen F. Borhegyi, "The Miraculous Shrines of Our Lord of

Esquipulas in Guatemala and Chimayo, New Mexico," *El Palacio* 63, no. 3 (March 1953): 8.

14. Hewett, *Pajarito Plateau*, 101.

15. Ibid., 102.

16. Ibid., 102-3.

17. Ibid., 103.

Chapter 4: Arizona

1. Lieutenant Joseph C. Ives, *Report upon the Colorado River of the West*, 36th Cong., 1861, 19.

2. Ibid., 64.

3. Ibid., 64.

4. Ibid., 71.

5. Ibid., 85.

6. Ibid., 86.

7. John Saul, "Circular Structures of Large Scale and Great Age on the Earth's Surface," *Nature* 271 (January 1978): 348.

Chapter 5: Nevada

1. "Sonorous Sand in Nevada," *Knowledge* 3 (1883): 64.

2. John F. Lindsay et al., "Sound-Producing Dune and Beach Sands," *Geological Society of America Bulletin* 87 (1976): 468.

3. George Washington Bean, "Report of George Washington Bean's Exploration in the South Western Deserts of Utah Territory, as given by himself to President Young," *Manuscript History of the Church, Brigham Young Period, 1844-1877*, Salt Lake City, Latter Day Saints Archives.

4. Lieutenant George M. Wheeler, *Preliminary Report: Explorations in Nevada and Arizona* (Washington, D.C.: Government Printing Office, 1872), 25.

Chapter 7: Washington

1. Victor Scheffer, "The Mystery of the Mima Mounds," *Scientific Monthly* 65 (1947): 283.

2. Howard E. Jackson, "The Mystery of the Mima Mounds," *Natural History* 65 (March 1956): 136-39, 162.

Chapter 9: Wyoming

1. S. A. Forbes, "A Preliminary Report on the Aquatic Invertebrate Fauna of the Yellowstone National Park," *Bulletin of the United States Fish Commission for 1891* (29 April 1893): 215.

2. Ferdinand Vandeveer Hayden, *Sixth Annual Report of the United States Geological and Geographical Survey of the Territories embracing Portions of Montana, Idaho, Wyoming, and Utah Being a Report of Progress of the Exploration for the year 1872* (Washington, D.C.: Government Printing Office, 1873), 234.

3. Edward Linton, in *Science* 22 (1893): 245.

4. Ibid., 246.

5. Ibid., 246.

6. Ibid., 246.

Bibliography

Abert, Lieutenant J. W. *Communicating a report of an expedition led by Lieutenant Abert on the upper Arkansas and through the country of the Camanche Indians in the fall of the year 1845—Journal of Lieutenant J. W. Abert from Bent's Fort to St. Louis in 1845.* 29th Cong., 1st sess., 1846. Doc. 438.

Alt, David D., and Donald W. Hyndman. *Roadside Geology of Idaho.* Missoula, Mont.: Mountain Press Publishing Company, 1991.

———. *Roadside Geology of Northern California.* Missoula, Mont.: Mountain Press Publishing Company, n.d.

———. *Roadside Geology of Washington.* Missoula, Mont.: Mountain Press Publishing Company, 1993.

Anderson, Alfred L. "Geology and Mineral Resources of Eastern Cassia County, Idaho." *Idaho Bureau of Mines and Geology Bulletin*, no. 14 (September 1931).

Baldwin, James D. *Ancient America in Notes on American Archaeology.* New York: Harper and Bros., 1872.

Bean, George Wasington. *Report of George Washington Bean's Exploration in the South Western Deserts of Utah Territory, as given by himself to President Young, June 7, 1858, Provo City, Utah County, Utah, in Manuscript History of the Church, Brigham Young Period, 1844-1877.* Salt Lake City, Utah: Latter Day Saints Archives.

Borhegyi, Stephen F. "The Miraculous Shrines of Our Lord of Esquipulas in Guatemala and Chimayo, New Mexico." *El Palacio* 63, no. 3 (March 1953).

Chronic, Halka. *Pages of Stone.* Seattle: The Mountaineers, 1986.

283

————. *Roadside Geology of New Mexico*. Missoula, Mont.: Mountain Press Publishing Company, 1987.

————. *Roadside Geology of Utah*. Missoula, Mont.: Mountain Press Publishing Company, 1991.

Corliss, William R. *Strange Artifacts*. Glen Arm, Md.: The Sourcebook Project, 1974.

————. *Unknown Earth*. Glen Arm, Md.: The Sourcebook Project, 1980.

————. *Handbook of Unusual Natural Phenomena*. Garden City, N.Y.: Anchor Press/Doubleday, 1983.

Downum, Christian E., and Todd W. Bostwick, eds. *Archaeology of the Pueblo Grande Platform Mound and Surrounding Features*. Vol. 1. Phoenix, Ariz.: Pueblo Grande Museum, 1993.

Dutton, Clarence. *Tertiary History of the Grand Canyon District with Atlas*. Washington, D.C.: Government Printing Office, 1851.

Ereira, Alan. *The Heart of the World*. London: Jonathan Cape, Ltd., 1990.

Fell, Barry. "Epigraphy of the Susquehanna Steles." *Occasional Publications of the Epigraphic Society* 2, no. 45 (May 1975): 1-8.

Fenn, Waldemar. *Grafica Prehistorica de Espana y El Origen de la Cultura Europea*. Menorca: M. Sintes Rotger, 1950.

Finch, John. "On the Celtic Antiquities of America." *American Journal of Science* 7 (1824): 149-61.

Forbes, S. A. "A Preliminary Report on the Aquatic Invertebrate Fauna of the Yellowstone National Park." *Bulletin of the United States Fish Commission for 1891* (April 29, 1893).

Fowke, Gerald. *Antiquities of Central and Southeastern Missouri*, Smithsonian Institution Bureau of American Ethnology, Bulletin 37. Washington, D.C.: Government Printing Office, 1910.

Gabelman, John W. "Cylindrical Structures in Permian (?) Siltstone, Eagle County, Colorado." *Journal of Geology* 63, no. 3 (1955): 214-27.

Goetzmann, William H. *Army Exploration in the American West: 1803-1863*. New Haven: Yale University Press, 1959.

————. *Exploration and Empire: The Explorer and the Scientist in the Winning of the American West*. New York: Alfred A. Knopf, 1966.

Goetzmann, William H., and Glyndwr Williams. *The Atlas of North American Exploration: From the Norse Voyages to the Race to the Pole*. New York: Prentice Hall, 1992.

Gordon, Cyrus H. *Before Columbus: Links between the Old World and Ancient America*. New York: Crown, 1971.

Hayden, Ferdinand Vandeveer. *Bulletin of the United States Geological and Geographical Survey of the Territories.* Vol. 2. Washington, D.C.: Government Printing Office, 1876.

————. *Sixth Annual Report of the United States Geological and Geographical Survey of the Territories embracing Portions of Montana, Idaho, Wyoming, and Utah Being a Report of Progress of the Exploration for the year 1872.* Washington, D.C.: Government Printing Office, 1873.

————. *Tenth Annual Report of the United States Geological and Geographical Survey of the Territories embracing Colorado and Parts of Adjacent Territories Being a Report of Progress of the Exploration for the year 1876.* Washington, D.C.: Government Printing Office, 1878.

Hewett, Edgar L. *Pajarito Plateau and its Ancient People.* Albuquerque: University of New Mexico Press, 1938.

Hewett, Edgar L., and Wayne L. Mauzy. *Landmarks of New Mexico.* Albuquerque: University of New Mexico Press, 1940.

Horsford, Cornelia. *An Inscribed Stone.* Cambridge, Mass.: Private printing, 1895.

Ives, Lieutenant Joseph C. *Report upon the Colorado River of the West.* 36th Cong., 1861.

Jackson, Howard E. "The Mystery of the Mima Mounds." *Natural History* 65 (March 1956): 136-39, 162.

Johnston, Brevet Lieutenant Colonel J. E., et al. *Reports of the Secretary of War with Reconnaissances of Routes from San Antonio to El Paso.* 31st Cong., Ex. Doc. 64, 1850.

Kay, Elizabeth. *Chimayo Valley Traditions.* Santa Fe, N.M.: Ancient City Press, 1987.

Kelsey, Joe. *Wyoming's Wind River Range.* Helena, Mont.: American Geographic Publishing, 1988.

Knechtel, Maxwell M. "Giant Playa-Crack Polygon in New Mexico Compared with Arctic Tundra-Crack Polygons." *American Geological Society of America Bulletin* 62 (1951): 1455.

Lageson, David R., and Darwin R. Spearing. *Roadside Geology of Wyoming.* Missoula, Mont.: Mountain Press Publishing Company, 1988.

Lang, Walter B. "Gigantic Drying Cracks in Animas Valley, New Mexico." *Science* 98, no. 2557 (December 31, 1943): 583-84.

Lindsay, John F., et al. "Sound-Producing Dune and Beach Sands." *Geological Society of America Bulletin* 87 (1976): 463-73.

Linton, Edward. *Science* 22 (1893): 245-46.

————. "Overhead Sounds of the Yellowstone Lake Region." *Science* 71 (1930): 97-99.

Lockley, Martin. *A Field Guide to Dinosaur Ridge*. Morrison, Colo.: Friends of Dinosaur Ridge, 1990.

Lubbock, John. *The Origins of Civilization and the Primitive Condition of Man*. New York: D. Appleton and Company, 1886.

Malville, J. McKimm, and Claudia Putnam. *Prehistoric Astronomy in the Southwest*. Boulder, Colo.: Johnson Books, 1989.

McGlone, William R., and Phillip M. Leonard. *Ancient Celtic America*. Fresno, Calif.: Panorama West Books, 1986.

McGlone, William R., et al. *Ancient American Inscriptions: Plowmarks or History?* Sutton, Mass.: Early Sites Research Society, 1993.

Merino, Enrique. "Self-Organization in Stylolites." *American Scientist* 80, no. 2 (September-October 1992): 466-73.

Mertz, Henriette. *Atlantis: Dwelling Place of the Gods*. Chicago: Private printing, 1976.

Noble, David Grant. *Ancient Ruins of the Southwest: An Archaeological Guide*. Flagstaff, Ariz.: Northland Publishing Co., 1991.

Parris, Lloyd E. *Caves of Colorado*. Boulder, Colo.: Pruett Publishing Company, 1973.

Patterson, Alex. *Rock Art Symbols of the Greater Southwest: A Field Guide*. Flagstaff, Ariz.: Northland Publishing Co., 1992.

Peet, Stephen D. *The Mound Builders: Their Works and Relics*. Chicago: Office of the American Antiquarian, 1892.

Pidgeon, William. *Traditions of De-coo-dah and Antiquarian Researches: Comprising Extensive Explorations, Surveys, and Excavations of the Wonderful and Mysterious Earthen Remains of the Mound Builders in America; the Traditions of the Last Prophet of the Elk Nation Relative to Their Origin and Use; and the Evidences of an Ancient Population More Numerous Than the Present Aborigines*. New York: Thayer, Bridgman and Fanning, 1853.

Pope, Maurice. *The Story of Archaeological Decipherment*. New York: Scribner, 1975.

Powell, John Wesley. *Exploration of the Colorado River of the West and Its Tributaries*. Washington, D.C.: Smithsonian Institution, Government Printing Office, 1875.

————. *The Ninth Annual Report of the Bureau of Ethnology to the Secretary of the Smithsonian Institution*. Washington, D.C.: Government Printing Office, 1892.

———. *The Twelfth Annual Report of the Bureau of Ethnology to the Secretary of the Smithsonian Institution*. Washington, D.C.: Government Printing Office, 1894.

Reader's Digest Association. *Earth's Mysterious Places*. Pleasantville, N.Y.: Reader's Digest Association, 1992.

Renaud, Etienne Bernardeau. *Archaeological Survey of Eastern Colorado, First Report*. Denver, Colo.: University of Denver, 1931.

———. *The Archaeological Survey of Colorado, Second Report*. Denver, Colo.: University of Denver, 1932.

———. *The Archaeological Survey of Colorado, Fourth Report, Seasons 1933 and 1934*. Denver, Colo.: University of Denver, 1935.

Rothovius, Andrew E. "The Celt-Culture of New England, First Millennium B.C." *NEARA Journal* 10, no. 2 (Summer-Fall 1975): 2-6.

Saul, John. "Circular Structures of Large Scale and Great Age on the Earth's Surface." *Nature* 271 (January 1978): 345-49.

Scheffer, Victor. "The Mystery of the Mima Mounds." *Scientific Monthly* 65 (1947): 283-94.

Schlee, John S. "Sandstone Pipes of the Laguna Area, New Mexico." *Journal of Sedimentary Petrology* 33, no. 1 (March 1963): 112-23.

Schmidt, Jeremy. *Lehman Caves*. Baker, Nev.: Great Basin Natural History Association, 1987.

Schoolcraft, Henry Rowe. *History of the Indian Tribes of the United States*. Philadelphia: J. B. Lippincott, 1857.

Simpson, Lieutenant J. H. "An Expedition into the Navajo Country." In *Reports of the Secretary of War with Reconnaissances of Routes from San Antonio to El Paso*. 31st Cong., Ex. Doc. 64, 1850.

Smith, Hugh M. "Mysterious Acoustic Phenomena in Yellowstone National Park." *Science* 63 (1926): 586-87.

"Sonorous Sand in Nevada." *Knowledge* 3 (1883): 63-64.

Sterling, Matthew. "Solving the Mystery of Mexico's Great Stone Spheres." *National Geographic Magazine* 136 (1969): 293-300.

Turney, Omar. "Prehistoric Irrigation in Arizona." In *Archaeology of the Pueblo Grande Platform Mound and Surrounding Features*. Vol. 1. Phoenix, Ariz.: Pueblo Grande Museum, 1993.

Unrau, Harlan D. *Basin and Range: A History of Great Basin National Park Nevada*. Baker, Nev.: U.S. Department of the Interior, National Park Service, 1990.

Van Ness, Margaret, et al. *Archaeological Survey and Test Excavation in the*

Turkey Canyon Area, Fort Carson Military Reservation, Pueblo and El Paso Counties, Colorado. Fort Collins, Colo.: Centennial Archaeology, Inc., 1990.

Vivian, A. Pendarves. *Wanderings in the Western Land.* London: Sampson Low, Marston, Searle & Rivington, 1880.

Washburn, A. L. "Classification of Patterned Ground and Review of Suggested Origins." *Bulletin of the Geological Society of America* 67 (July 1956): 823-66.

Wheeler, Lieutenant George M. *Preliminary Report: Explorations in Nevada and Arizona.* Washington, D.C.: Government Printing Office, 1872.

———. *U.S. Geographical Surveys West of the 100th Meridian: Reports.* 7 vols. Washington, D.C.: Government Printing Office, 1876-1879.

Wilson, Daniel. *Prehistoric Annals of Scotland.* 2 vols. London: Macmillan, 1863.

Winchell, Alexander. *Sketches of Creation.* New York: Harper & Brothers, 1870.

———. *Geological Excursions.* 3rd ed. Chicago: S. C. Griggs & Company, 1886.

Wyckoff, Jerome. *Rock Scenery of the Hudson Highlands and Palisades.* Glens Falls, N.Y.: Adirondack Mountain Club, 1971.

Zier, Christian J., et al. *Historic Preservation Plan for Fort Carson Military Reservation, Colorado.* Fort Collins, Colo.: Centennial Archaeology, Inc., 1987.

Index